Journeys
Australian Women in Mexico

Journeys
Australian Women in Mexico

Compiled
and edited by

Ruth Adler
Jacqueline Buswell
Jenny Cooper

Riverton
Press

Journeys
Australian Women in Mexico

Compiled and edited by Ruth Adler, Jacqueline Buswell and Jenny Cooper.

First published in 2021 by Riverton Press, Sydney, New South Wales, Australia.

This book is copyright. Apart from any fair dealing for the purpose of private study, research, criticism or review, as permitted under the Copyright Act 1968, no part may be reproduced by any process without written permission. Enquiries should be made to the publisher at info@rivertonpress.com or to the editors at ozwomenmexico@gmail.com.

Copyright © of each contribution belongs to the author, 2021.
Copyright © of this collection belongs to Riverton Press, 2021.

ISBN paperback: 978-0-6482305-8-8
ISBN epub: 978-0-6482305-9-5
ISBN mobi: 978-0-6450335-0-2

Cover image by Manon Saur.
Photo of cover artwork by John Davies.
Book design by Mutare, Ciudad de México, México.

First published with the financial support of the Australian Embassy in Mexico.

Contents

9   Acknowledgements
11 Introduction

ASTONISHING MEXICO

15 **Mexico, new world** ✻ Jacqueline Buswell
27 **Heaven and Earth** ✻ Jacqueline Buswell
29 **The earthquake** ✻ Ruth Adler
37 **Still here** ✻ Jenny Cooper

JOURNEYS

51   **Learning in Mexico** ✻ Raewyn Connell
63   **On the track of the elusive B. Traven** ✻ Heidi Zogbaum
71   **The posting** ✻ Ruth Adler
87   **Tijuana freeway** ✻ Jacqueline Buswell
89   **Mexico remembered** ✻ Lilit Thwaites
97   **My journey to *Misión México* and beyond** ✻ Pamela Jean Skuse
103 **Cathy Carey: A tribute** ✻ Jenny Cooper
111 **Just dancing** ✻ Jacqueline Buswell

113 **Peg Job: A tribute** ✳ Jacqueline Buswell
115 **Livin' la vida loca** ✳ Lulu Honeywild
121 **What not to do** ✳ Jennifer Perkin
127 **True story** ✳ Jacqueline Buswell

LOVE STORIES

131 **My life in Mexico** ✳ Manon Saur
147 **Magical** ✳ Jacqueline Buswell
149 *Camino de flores* ✳ Rachael Byrne
157 **Little things of nothing** ✳ Jenny Pollak
159 **Extracts from correspondence between Luis Vidal and Jenny Pollak, 1988-1989** ✳ Jenny Pollak
171 **A green chilli sauce made from tomatoes** ✳ Jenny Pollak
175 **Pilgrimages** ✳ Jeannie Lewis
191 **Land of corn** ✳ Jacqueline Buswell
195 **White rabbits** ✳ Jenny Pollak
197 **Between** ✳ Jenny Pollak
199 **The expats** ✳ Ruth Adler

Acknowledgements

The editors would like to thank all the contributors to this anthology for freely sharing their stories. We are very grateful to the Australian Embassy in Mexico for its support and generous financial assistance for the publication of *Journeys*, in particular, Bernard Unkles, Deputy Head of Mission and Counsellor, and Lorena Zapiain, Public Diplomacy Officer. We also extend our thanks and appreciation to Ricardo Gallardo Sánchez of *Mutare* for his creative input and excellent suggestions regarding the book's design and to Manon Saur for her imagination and insight in creating the image for the book's cover. We acknowledge our families and friends for their enthusiastic support for this project and for encouraging us to bring what began as an idea among a few friends to this collection of stories, poems, letters, song lyrics and reflections.

Introduction

Journeys: Australian Women in Mexico seeks to capture the experiences of thirteen Australian women who have lived, or are currently living, in Mexico or have some attachment to the country. The contributors to this book differ in age, their motives for travelling to Mexico and the time frame of their contact with the country: their stories, poems, letters, song lyrics and reflections span a period of 50 years since the 1970s. They look back on their experiences with varying mixtures of nostalgia, pleasure and pain. One set up a business, another established a refuge and surf project for children, and another undertook gender transition between her visits and so experienced the country on new terms. Our contributors include academics, poets, a diplomat, a singer, a model and women who went to Mexico to accompany or meet a partner. And sadly, two Australians who might have participated in this book have died, so we have written tributes to them.

Many of the contributors have not written previously about their Mexican experiences and impressions. Given the opportunity to express themselves on their involvement with Mexico, these authors have conveyed through their writing how much they have enjoyed reliving their time there. The collection is a testimony to the diversity and richness of long-standing personal links between Australia and

Mexico, and we hope that the reader will enjoy this insight into Mexican culture that is not to be found in classic travel books.

The idea for the book arose as a spontaneous response to an academic treatise by a young Mexican author, Mónica Laura Vázquez Maggio, titled *Mobility Patterns and Experiences of the Middle Classes in a Globalizing Age: The Case of Mexican Migrants in Australia* (Springer International Publishing, 2017). Over a glass of wine in Canberra with some friends who had met in Mexico, somebody suggested somewhat flippantly 'Why don't we write about our experiences in Mexico?' The invitation to participate was by word of mouth, until the Australian Embassy in Mexico published a call for submissions on its Facebook page in October 2019.

Astonishing Mexico highlights the impression of first visits to Mexico and the impact of events which the writers had not previously experienced. *Journeys* documents the interaction of the authors with Mexico as a result of academic research or travel, work or business, and/or involvement with cultural and political issues. *Love stories* are well, just that and all of that, love stories.

Astonishing Mexico

Mexico, new world

Jacqueline Buswell

JACQUELINE BUSWELL was born in Wagga Wagga, New South Wales, and completed a Bachelor of Arts at the Australian National University. She lived in Mexico for more than 20 years, in Mexico City and in Tepoztlán, Morelos. Jacqueline has worked as a journalist, teacher of English as a second language, and Spanish-English translator and interpreter. She completed a Masters in Creative Writing at the University of Sydney in 2011. Ginninderra Press published her first book of poems, *Song of a Journeywoman*, in 2013. Jacqueline established Riverton Press in 2018 and has recently published a new book of poetry, *sprinting on quicksand*.

The sky was showing off a magnificent sunset, with the west reflected in the eastern clouds, where there seemed to be two snow-tipped mountains. This was my first glimpse of the very real and live volcano Popocatépetl and its 'partner' Ixtaccíhuatl, and I mistook them for clouds. So great, my ignorance of Mexican geography, vulcanology! El Popo is a perfect and active volcanic cone, and beside it lies the Sleeping Woman mountain, stuff of mythology of course, hero and maiden...

This was the first of many experiences of shifting realities in Mexico, it happened just a few days after arrival, when I was wandering the mundane streets near the southern bus station at Taxqueña. An introductory example of contrasts with my known world – Mexico City is more or less as high as Australia's highest mountain, and the population of the greater metropolitan area is greater than that of all Australia.

A few months later, workers digging near the Zócalo for some urban improvement found the Moon Goddess Coyolxauhqui. She was carved on a round stone more than three metres in diameter. A member of warring Aztec deity families, Coyolxauhqui was killed, dismembered and her head was thrown to the sky. She thus became a moon goddess, though some say she belonged to the stars of the Milky Way.

I was thrilled because she was a goddess, but it was exciting too for the archaeologists, as this was a fantastic discovery right at city centre, at the site of the siege of the Grand Tenochtitlan, where the Aztecs held out for months against the Spaniards in 1521. Eight years later we could see the stone for ourselves when the Great Temple Museum was opened.

It took me some time to appreciate Mexico's many layers and the complexity of its history and society. The layers were visible enough: giant Olmec heads, Mayan, Zapotec, Aztec pyramids, Spanish churches and palaces, elegant colonial buildings in the red volcanic rock *tezontle,* indigenous adobe housing, shacks of tar-coated cardboard, glass constructions like the Stock Exchange (monument to capitalism).

The ancient peoples had their gods, myths and social hierarchies, and the Spanish invasion by Cross and Spade did not extinguish many of those deep-seated traditions during three centuries of colonial rule. Native Mexicans and Creoles alike fought for and won independence in 1821, and entered a quandary over Nationalism and Europeanism. Another hundred years passed before the Revolution when perhaps a million people died.

In the democracy established after that, one political party held power for nearly seventy years. Speaking in Mexico City in 1990, Peruvian writer Mario Vargas Llosa described the system as a 'perfect dictatorship' (and left town the next day). For there was a perceptible shadow and sadness marking the psyche of the country and eroding the exercise of freedom. In 1968, just before the Mexican Olympics, government troops attacked student protests and killed some 400 people at the *Plaza de las Tres Culturas* in Tlatelolco, and imprisoned many students, workers and intellectuals for several years. There was another tragedy like this in 1971 at the Polytechnic Institute in Mexico

City, and armed guerrilla warfare was waged in the state of Guerrero in that decade. In fact, one always had to stop at one or more military roadblocks entering that state.

The contrasts between rich and poor were easy to see: high walls of the houses with gardens and art collections, and across the road, zones where families carry in their water and let the grey waters flow onto the street. It took longer to perceive other human rights violations, the racism against indigenous peoples even while their ancient cultures were exalted, and to read, see, hear the richness of poetic, artistic and musical expressions – surrealism, social realism and much else beyond and in between.

Firstly of course, I had to learn the language! I had a little school French and Latin, but all I knew of Spanish when I arrived in Mexico was *gracias*, and the old cliché that Mexicans left everything for *mañana*.

A visit to the Anthropology Museum is an over-whelming introduction to Mexican history and culture and I won't attempt to describe it here. I'll just mention a poem by the ancient poet Netzahualcoyotl, an extract from which is engraved at the Museum entrance, and which puts things in perspective:

> *Yo Nezahualcóyotl lo pregunto:*
> *¿Acaso de veras se vive con raíz en la tierra?*
> *Nada es para siempre en la tierra: Sólo un poco aquí.*
> *Aunque sea de jade se quiebra, Aunque sea de oro se rompe,*
> *Aunque sea plumaje de quetzal se desgarra.*
> *No para siempre en la tierra:*
> *Sólo un poco aquí.*
> This is Nezahualcóyotl. My question is,
> Do we really have any roots on this earth?
> Nothing on earth is forever: just a short time here.
> Even if it's made of jade, it breaks, even gold fractures,
> Even the quetzal feather is torn.
> Not forever on this earth: only a short time here.

In Mexico I never forgot the sense of space I knew from Australia, but I came to know that I was just part of the masses. I used the metro a lot; it was built by the French and the wagons were bright orange with rubber tyres. Most but not all of it was underground. Some four million people were said to use the metro every day. Three memorable interchange stations were Balderas, Pino Suárez and La Raza. Passageways were filled with commuters, jam packed but moving. A pyramid was found during the construction of the Pino Suárez station, it was dedicated to one of my favourites, the god of wind Ehécatl. His task, obviously, was to provide air to the underground. La Raza featured extensive corridors where one could meditate on walking a mile in another's shoes. Metro Balderas was honoured in a love song of that name by rock star Rockdrigo, who died in his apartment during the 1985 earthquake.

And if I wasn't learning about the vulnerability of masses fast enough, there was always help from a dear flatmate who pasted a certain photo on a cupboard door. The picture showed a crowd being crushed against a cyclone fence at a football stadium in England. Death by crushing; fright and horror written on the close-up of a young woman. My flatmate didn't want to tell me to avoid crowds; she was just morbidly fascinated by the terrors of human existence.

The 1985 earthquakes were by far the most traumatic geological/social event I have experienced. And yet, where I lived in southern Mexico City, not even the salt shaker fell off the shelf. I was a journalist at the time, with a pass issued by the all-powerful Presidency of the Nation, and I was amazed and disturbed to be given access to areas by soldiers who closed the way to people who really wanted and needed to get to a certain spot. Collapsed buildings, rubble, dust, displacements, loss of family, loss of homes. Stunning rescues. A powerful solidarity shown by residents helping each other. The statistics battle between official sources and others about how many people died. Four thousand? Forty thousand? Some years later, I wrote a poem, you can read it below.

REBELLION IN CHIAPAS

On New Year's Day in 1994 Mexico woke to the Zapatista Revolution in the southern state of Chiapas. Armed men and women in balaclavas had taken several towns overnight and declared their rejection of bad government, and the following demands for the rights of indigenous people: *techo, tierra, trabajo, pan, salud*. To give the full list: housing, land, work, bread, health, education, independence, democracy, freedom, justice and peace, with dignity.

While the government sent out the Army in response, popular support for the indigenous cause was so strong and widespread that rulers had to change tactics and start negotiations. Many years of talks and government betrayals on accords followed, including military attacks by the Army. The uprising was accompanied by the writings of *subcomandante* Marcos, a non-indigenous man whose words were imaginative, humorous and inspiring, and provided a unique theoretical base and publicity campaign. Thousands of people, including well known artists, writers, militants from many countries, visited the Zapatista communities to show their support, to join in meetings and conferences to plan the new world where 'for everyone, everything'.

I had visited Chiapas before the uprising and I visited two or three times after. Once I travelled with a musician from the women's circus, the English Camilla. She carried her accordion in a heavy rigid box, but it was truly worth it when she played to the barefooted children in a Zapatista community. Camilla had previously given workshops to children in Mexico City and Guatemala, teaching them how to make and play instruments from materials like discarded plastic tubes, buckets, bottles.

STORY OF A VILLAGE

I had never lived in a small town before, and I couldn't have chosen a more special and different kind of a town for exploring a micro cosmos. I had a part-time existence there for the most part, commuting weekly to Mexico City for work, but I also enjoyed four or five years as a full time resident.

Tepoztlán in 1978 was still a picturesque village, with cobblestone streets, adobe houses, 16th century churches, its surrounding mountains opening down to the hot plains of southern Morelos. It had the makings of what it has become, a small town overwhelmed by its attractiveness. To give you an idea, streets that used to be quiet and pretty are now busy thoroughfares, and the main bus stop has been moved away from the centre.

Part of its attraction lies in its proximity to Mexico City, making it easy for people to have weekend homes there, or make short visits. Another attraction is the climate, best in the world... warm sunny days, cooling down at night thanks to the altitude. The rainy season can be thrilling with heavy downpours and fantastic electrical storms.

It has its native-born population (known as *tepoztecos*) and those from outside – from other parts of Mexico and overseas, who are equally considered foreigners by the locals. If the outsiders remain in the town long enough, they become *tepoztizos*. In spite of or because of its significant foreign population, *tepoztecos* are fiercely nationalistic about their town. Not so much about their land, of which they have sold a large amount to the foreigners.

The mountain cliffs are infinitely textured and beautiful, green and wondrous in the rainy season, especially when mist and clouds filter through the range. In the dry season, cliff colours change with the sun, brown, red, coppery. They are a special delight during the peak of the dry, around April, when purple jacarandas contrast against the rock, and help the soul endure water scarcities.

The god Tepozteco or Tepoztécatl, god of pulque (a fermented alcoholic drink made from the maguey plant) presumably has his residence near the pyramid built in his honour at the top of the mountain. The ascent is rather arduous and takes an hour for the average visitor. On the night of his fiesta on 8 September, the best and bravest of those favoured by the god manage to get up and perhaps down the mountain, even in the rain, with the warmth of an alcoholic beverage inside them. In March the pyramid is also visited by many, generally of the *tepoztizo* and foreigner tribes, dressed in white for the spring equinox.

The foreigner population in Tepoztlán was eclectic and exotic. Sure, it had the weekend bankers, diplomats and intellectuals from Mexico City, but there was plenty more. During the years I lived in a small cul-de-sac with five houses, my neighbours included two Spanish and one French single mothers of small children, three Japanese women, one a young mother with her weekend Mexican partner who had established his *casa chica* next door, an Irish journalist and her American husband, a violin maker from the US, three bourgeois lesbians from Mexico City, a single Mexican woman from a Lebanese family, and a Mexican indigenous couple, dancers in the Conchero movement. As all these came and went, there was one permanent Mexican family from Mexico City who came every weekend, until one of their daughters came to live there permanently.

Beyond this little street there were always many Italians in town, some fleeing the difficult Red Brigade years of the 70s, others breaking a drug addiction, others, just travelling. One year a women's circus came to town, it was made up of eight women from the UK and the US. They stayed for a month and prepared their acrobatic, juggling, music and clown acts, then travelled to Nicaragua to support the Sandinista revolution. They gave a couple of performances before they left, and proved that a circus does not have to enslave animals to offer a good show. The bearded lady of the group broke her arm while practising the tight rope, so switched her skills to playing the clarinet, successfully joining the flute, trombone and drum.

The town is made up of *barrios*, each with its 16th century church; Santo Domingo, la Santísima Trinidad, San Sebastián, San Miguel being some central ones. The municipality also consists of several outlying villages, and these generally conserve their Nahuatl names as well as the Christian saint: Santiago Tepetlapa, San Juan Tlacotenco, Santo

Domingo Ocotitlán. And then there is Amatlán de Quetzalcóatl, said to be the birthplace of the feathered serpent god of morning/evening (Venus).

Each *barrio* has its fiesta to honour its patron saint and families take turns to cook and cater for any visitor who cares to come, foreigners included. The meal will generally include turkey served with the famous chocolate-based mole sauce, rice, beans and tortillas. The community generosity is astounding. My friends Michele and Melissa studied local traditional medicine for several years with a healer, Doña Paula. When I say, study, it would be more correct to say they did a kind of apprenticeship as part of the family. So, as well as learning how to diagnose, give massages and herbal medicines, they helped on the fiestas, cooking and serving meals.

The soundtrack to every *fiesta de barrio* consisted of fireworks known as *cohetes*, rockets, loud bangs that go off at any time of the day or night, especially at dawn to remind us, we have a new day, a new party. Only at Carnival would the rocket makers go to the trouble of creating visual fireworks, with castles and spinners and bull runners.

The Carnival highlight is dancing in the square each evening with the *chinelos*, who dress in long black velvet robes and masks, large colourful head pieces, embroidered or painted, beaded and bearded. Everyone is welcome to dance to the music of local bands playing wind instruments, the steps are easy to follow, and round and round the square the world goes in a trance.

Interest in the esoteric was always high in Tepoztlán, among *tepoztecos* and *tepoztizos* alike, and conversations often turned to astrology, UFOs, weird inexplicable occurrences, traditional healing practices. We read the I Ching, the Tarot, the Runes, we argued about the fatality associated with readings by certain astrologers, and whether the stars determined destiny or left us room for free choice.

Traditional medicine played an important role in Mexican society and medicinal plants were and are investigated in various institutions across the country. Traditional healing methods also included massages, and concepts like the evil eye. There were cleansings by local healers done by passing certain herbs or an egg over the body. The egg was then broken and diagnosis was made according to the appearance of the yolk and albumen. The corn crop was traditionally protected in late September by a cross made of the plant *pericón*. These crosses of yellow flowers were also placed on houses and even cars to protect one from evil spirits. This plant is known to the scientists as *Tagetes lucida*, and has antiseptic properties.

Tepoztlán has a river, Río Atongo. During my early years there, this was a polluted non-functioning ditch most of the time, though when it had water women would wash clothes at a point near Ixcatepec. That area was littered with chlorine bottles, and the water unfortunately also got 'whitened'. There was an elderly Belgian or Dutch man who took it upon himself to save the river, and he constructed a few walls of stone as dikes so water could accumulate near some grand old cypress (*ahuehuete*) trees. Various governments determined he had no right to interfere with the river and knocked down the dikes. He would build again, request permission, negotiate... After several years the walls were allowed to remain. The first job was to remove the rubbish collected at these dikes. To prevent rubbish being thrown in at that spot, a statue of the Virgin of Guadalupe was positioned to protect it. She worked well. Towards the end of his life, that man – and the rest of us – had the joy of witnessing small regattas in the river pool. This was a lesson that one single person can make a difference.

The town's market place is the roofless main square. Rain or shine. For days of grand fiesta such as the Carnival, the marketers have to move and it's difficult to find your favourite merchant – under the ferris wheel perhaps. The main market days are Wednesday and Sunday when sellers come from outlying areas with home grown products, or material from the forest like firewood kindling and charcoal. Crafts persons set up their stalls, especially on Sundays, to provide a magnificent selection of Mexican art and craft – embroideries, weavings, jewellery, hammocks, artwork on hand-made paper, masks, artefacts for each seasonal feast... On these days the market would extend down *Avenida Revolución* and around the corner almost to the Carlos Pellicer Museum.

The market was a great place to eat all sorts of corn-based foods, *tacos, tlacoyos, sopes, quesadillas, tamales, pozole* and more. Over my years in Mexico, I used to joke, my gut changed from being a child of wheat to become an adoptive child of corn. I loved to roam the outskirts of Tepoztlán where the local farmers still cultivated their *milpas* – corn with beans, squash and flowers. While my poem Tijuana Freeway is about migration, the last part refers to the home base – the cornfield, and the fire for making tortillas.

THE GOLF CLUB WAR

The greatest battle fought in Tepoztlán during my years in Mexico was the conflict about the *Club de Golf*. Businessmen from the state capital Cuernavaca, with the support of the state government, wanted to build a golf course on land they had acquired some decades before. The *tepoztecos* said they didn't play golf, didn't know what golf was and did not want a golf course. Months of demonstrations, blockades, violence. People on both sides were killed. Tepoztlán Municipality declared itself an independent entity and no longer recognised the State government.

One Saturday morning I was driving into town and was stopped at a road block manned by anti-golf clubbers who were armed with paint and brushes and a few long sticks serving as weapons. I stopped, I had to stop, and they scrawled two slogans on the car: 'No to the golf club' and something else, I forget. They also hit the car with their clubs and gave it a dint. Then a person with sense intervened, told them to stop, told me to go. I was thankful they didn't write 'Death to the Governor' on the car. I agreed with the town's opposition to the golf club, but I hated the way members of the movement became so incensed as to wish death upon their opponents.

Finally, the businessmen said they no longer wanted to invest there. But then it took months for the state and the municipality to sort out relations. Later there have been similar conflicts – not so bloody perhaps – about highway extensions at the cost of forests.

ONLY A SHORT TIME HERE

Leaving Tepoztlán, leaving Mexico after 22 years, was one huge wrench, but it seemed the right thing to do at the time. I used to say, I won't leave Mexico until I understand it, though one of my Japanese neighbours used to say, you don't 'understand' Mexico, you just have to 'get it'. I had moved up into the mountains and came to feel too young for such a retreat; I wanted more world. I organised a garage sale, then another. When the car was gone I was ready to buy a ticket, and bought a one-way fare to New York. The rest, as they say, is another story…

Heaven and Earth

Jacqueline Buswell

The sky flares crimson. It wakes me.
When I look again the show
has closed and solace fled
from the pillow. The quake begins
at 7.19 and lasts nearly
two minutes. Moving in circles
and waves somewhere
near nine on Richter, the tremor
shatters the spines of scores of
buildings which collapse like
broken sandwiches. Five hundred
seamstresses locked in a sweatshop
on San Antonio Abad perish together.
Mothers who try to cross
the buckling rooms to reach infants
do not get there till the quake ceases.
The second tremor comes
eighteen hours later
escalating the dust and panic
of the searching and the weeping.
Even two weeks on, people are found

alive under the rubble. And in all
those days of tears we hardly see
the sky – though many would speak
to the god they believe there,
imploring or imprecating.
Finally we notice, for it is
unusual: each day beams clear
autumn sunshine and we see why
our smog-clouded mountain-circled
city once was named the most
transparent region of the air.

The earthquake

Ruth Adler

RUTH ADLER was born in Melbourne and completed a Doctor of Philosophy (PhD) degree in Mexican history and politics at La Trobe University's Institute of Latin American Studies in 1991. Ruth was a senior career officer with the Australian Department of Foreign Affairs and Trade until 2016 and served at the Australian Embassy in Mexico City as Deputy Head of Mission between 1998 and 2000. Ruth first went to Mexico in 1985 to undertake research for her PhD and was in the centre of Mexico City when an earthquake of 8.1 magnitude struck at 7.19am on Thursday 19 September 1985.

I am asleep in my bed on the third floor of the run-down two star Maria Angelo Hotel in the Colonia Cuauhtémoc. I awake to feel my rickety bed shaking violently backwards and forwards. For a moment, I think there is someone in the room, shaking the bed. As I become conscious, I see the light above my bed swinging and I realise it is an earthquake. I have never been in an earthquake and I recall a US television show I had once seen which advised that one should stand in the doorway. I jump out of bed, open the door of my room and, in my nightie, clasp the two sides of the door frame. The building lurches and creaks in all directions and a church bell clangs to the rhythm of the quake; I hang on for my life.

In the distance, I hear people shouting in Spanish, 'it's an earthquake!' I stand in my doorway, not afraid, but somehow paralysed. After what seems like several minutes, the earth ceases to move. Adrenalin surges through my body and I am relieved to be alive.

I dress quickly and go down two flights of stairs to the hotel lobby. Pancho, the 30-something year old night manager of the hotel, says *'hay miles de muertos'*. There are thousands of dead, but – apart from a couple of broken windows – our hotel is okay. I step into the street; the power lines are down and they spark and fizzle in the slimy, wet drains of our street, Rio Lerma.

'¡*Cuidado señorita*! It's dangerous out there,' shouts Pancho.

I ignore him and step into the middle of the road. All cars have stopped and people step-out of randomly parked vehicles, confused and bewildered. In the distance, I hear sirens – a sound that will continue incessantly for several days to come. On the other side of the road, a woman sits on a low stool, with a baby wrapped in a shawl on her back. She is cooking fried tacos over a small fire. I am suddenly very hungry. I buy two tacos; hot melted cheese oozes out as I eat them from a piece of brown paper. It seems like the best food I have ever had. There is something very calming about the sight of this woman, making her tacos as chaos unfolds around her. A small queue of people forms in front of her; people still need to eat and I slip away.

At the hotel, Pancho has the radio on and we learn that there has just been an earthquake of 8.1 magnitude. People are told to report damage to the local authorities and to remain at home. We learn that the metro service has been temporarily suspended while it is inspected for damage and the golden statue of the Angel of Independence on the Reforma has not fallen, unlike in the 1957 earthquake. Things cannot be as bad as they were in 1957.

I walk two blocks to the Reforma and see a partially collapsed office building, dust billowing from the rubble. A few people stand outside, arms folded, heads down and pacing anxiously, but there is no sign of rescue workers. I wonder who might be trapped inside at this early hour. In the distance, I see the Angel, a somehow reassuring sight.

I walk towards the historic centre of the city to find out whether the only other person I know in Mexico – a landlady who had thrown me onto the street on the previous Sunday morning following a dispute over rent – had survived. I walk past the Alameda Park, past the rubble of the Regis Hotel and several other buildings which have collapsed. People cluster in groups, sobbing that there are people trapped in buildings. Men pull at the rubble with their bare hands; I wonder where the authorities and official rescue workers are. I feel helpless and wish I could help.

I reach Calle Tacuba where I lived briefly with my landlady. The ancient, dilapidated building is still intact and I think better of ringing the bell to the tiny fourth floor apartment where she lived with her 14 year old daughter. She is alive; that is all I need to know.

I keep walking to the Zócalo, Mexico City's main square. Mexico's national cathedral and the national palace appear to be unscathed. The square is, however, surrounded by armed military officers and trucks and tanks. A man desperately tries to get across the square and a couple of officers raise their rifles. I wonder why these soldiers are not helping with the rescue effort. Are they protecting the national palace? Are they afraid of looting or riots?

I am suddenly struck by the gravity of the situation and make my way back to the hotel. There is no water or power in the hotel and people have drifted in from the streets, people who have become homeless as a result of the quake. Pancho asks me would I share my room with a stranger. Sure, I say. He asks whether I will return to Australia. That has not occurred to me and, in any case, there is no way of getting out of Mexico City. I tell him that I plan to stay and continue with my research once things settle.

We bunker down for a long night terrified of the prospect of an aftershock. I am invited to the room of a Mexican woman, Mariela, who I realise lives permanently in the hotel. Mariela is in her 30s and wears tight jeans, boots, costume jewellery and bright red lipstick. Her black hair is pulled back. Her room is like a boudoir and I wonder what she does for a living. She is curious about me, we chat and are later joined by an older Mexican man (is he her pimp?) and a down-at-heel Californian by the name of Dan, who lives in Mexico City, but does not have a home. I am reminded of George Orwell's *Down and Out in Paris and London*. We talk for most of the night, share biscuits, fruit and tequila, and briefly bond. They can't understand what a young Australian woman like me is doing alone in Mexico City and want to know if I have a Mexican boyfriend yet.

At Dan's suggestion, the next day I make contact with the Australian embassy. They tell me that they are compiling a list of Australians in Mexico that they will send to the Department of Foreign Affairs in Canberra, which will contact families. They tell me I have done the right thing getting in touch. I learn that two Australians – two Mexican government scholarship students who had arrived in Mexico City the night before the earthquake – were in the Hotel Regis when it collapsed. One was believed to have been killed and the other, Rod – who had been on the sixth floor – had survived and walked away from the rubble, with only his jeans and passport. He had been found wandering in the street by a kind local who pointed him in the direction of the embassy.

Later that day I meet Rod and we go shopping to buy him a toothbrush, toothpaste and a few basics. Someone in the embassy has lent him some clothes. That night we end up in Polanco, with Steve, a First Secretary in the embassy. We have pizza and beer. We feel relaxed, almost happy, and recount our earthquake stories. Rod is amazed to be still alive and somewhat shocked; he has not yet developed the survivor's guilt which will later haunt him.

As we tuck into our pizza, the second quake comes; this time the magnitude is 7.5. We look at each other, grab our beers and run onto the street. Perhaps foolishly, we sit in the middle of the road, but it seems like the safest place to be. Buildings sway and the earth moves underneath us. We are silent, as we wait for it to stop. Once it is safe to move, we return to the restaurant. The owner says he is closing-up for the night; we offer to pay, but he refuses to accept the money. 'You couldn't finish your meal properly,' he smiles. We are touched by his generosity.

Steve asks me how I will get back to my hotel. I say that I will be fine and hop into the first taxi which comes along. The taxi takes me about two hundred metres and stops.

'I can't take you any further. I have to leave you here. I won't charge you,' the driver says. I plead with him to take me further, but to no avail.

I am stranded and have no idea where I am. I walk aimlessly for a few minutes and then realise I am on the edge of Mexico City's main park, Chapultepec Park. But where in Chapultepec Park am I? There is no street lighting, it is pitch black. I see a large number of people drifting in one direction across the park. I have no idea where they are going, but I decide to follow them. After all, it is better to be around people than to be completely alone in this huge park.

I walk for an hour, maybe two. Even though I am surrounded by people, I feel completely alone and afraid. I reach the other side of the park and realise that I have come out onto the Reforma. As I walk along the Reforma, I see that a tent city has sprung-up. Hundreds of people are camped on the Reforma because they are either homeless or too afraid to return to their homes. These tent cities for the homeless – *los damnificados* – will be a feature of the city for many months as the Mexican government struggles with the aftermath. Within half an hour, I am back at the hotel.

'Where were you?' asks Dan. 'We were worried about you.'

I explain what had happened and we settle into Mariela's room for the night. We still have no water nor electricity in the hotel and again share the few things we have. I realise that my parents and family will be desperately worried about me, but in the era before cell phones, the internet and Facebook, I have no way of contacting them. Someone mentions that the Mexican telephone company – Telmex – has survived the quake and that it is not too far away; maybe I could try to call my parents from there?

The next day, I arrive to a queue of several hundred people and take my place. We are told that there will be a wait of four to six hours and that each individual can make one free call of a maximum of three minutes. I wait. Suddenly there is an announcement: *'No hay llamadas a Israel'* – there are no calls to Israel. A few people drop out of the line, throw up their hands and sigh – I feel sorry for them.

My turn finally comes and I am passed a piece of paper on which I write my parents' number in Sydney. I am told to wait in a booth and pick up the phone. A voice says, 'this is Mexico calling' and I am through to my parents. I feel overcome and momentarily wish I could be back home. My parents have been frantically worried, the phone has not stopped ringing and they have had no way of getting any news. A brother of mine who works at American Express had tried to find out if he could make contact with me through the company; all he was able to find out was that the American Express building in Mexico City had not collapsed. The time for my call is up, I have to go. My parents tell me to be careful.

Over the next few days, I learn that the official death toll is of the order 5,000, with several hundred buildings collapsed. Some estimates put the death toll at around 20,000. Nancy Reagan visits and delivers a 'letter of sympathy' from President Reagan and a $US1 million 'down-payment' on disaster relief for Mexico. Hundreds of people have died in Tlatelolco, a large apartment building complex close to the Plaza of Three Cultures in the north of Mexico City, and the Centro Médico hospital has collapsed, leaving hundreds dead and injured. Remarkably, almost a week after the earthquake, a number of newborn babies are pulled from the rubble of the hospital. The city is collectively overjoyed with the news.

The tents cities persist, photos of missing loved ones are plastered on the metro, in stations and in the street, and the slow process of rebuilding begins. Time seems to divide into two periods: before and after the earthquake and most conversations inevitably drift to where people were on the day of the earthquake. People are haunted by dreams of being trapped in buildings and unable to escape, and the slightest earth tremor instils fear and anxiety. I have recurrent dreams of earthquakes and being trapped in buildings for years to come. Everyone knows someone who has suffered some loss. A collective sense of what would now be described as post-traumatic stress sets in, as people relive their experiences. It will be many years before things return to 'normal'.

Still here

Jenny Cooper

JENNY COOPER, Jennifer Ann Cooper Tory on her official Mexican documents, grew up in Bankstown, New South Wales. She taught in Australian high schools until December 1968 when she left to explore the world. Jenny has now retired after first teaching English, then Gender and Economics, at the National Autonomous University of Mexico for over forty years. She currently lives in Santiago Tepetlapa, Morelos, with her husband Juan, but pursues her grandchildren around the globe whenever the opportunity presents itself.

> 'There's nowhere you can be that isn't where you're meant to be.'
> *John Lennon*

I first landed in Mexico in December of 1968 by accident. Had the Suez Canal not been closed because of the war with Egypt, my two friends and I would not have sailed to England from Australia through the Panama Canal. Our travel agent suggested that from Panama we could take a bus overland for a side trip to Mexico, which we did. After two months of playing tourists we returned to Panama, took our passenger boat, the Fair Sky and sailed to London. My world had opened up and I wanted more. The incident I describe here is an excerpt taken from my autoethnographic memoir in progress.

It's so cold I can't control my teeth or my knees. But is it the cold or my nerves which make my body shudder, my teeth to chatter and my knees to knock? I'm wearing a miniskirt and a thin white cotton blouse.

And the darkness, as in a jammed lift in a blackout. I try to get a hold of myself. What had that yoga teacher said? Breathe deeply, inhale one, two; exhale out, three, four. This helps. I sit still for a moment and try to focus. My eyes become accustomed to the blackness. The silhouettes of Juan, my *compañero*, and our Peruvian friend (affectionately known as *la negra Emilia*) emerge, the three of us perched on the edge of a concrete bench. The cold filters through the fat on my thighs which begin to burn. In the distance I can also make out a desk and some agents huddled under a cone of light as though they were plotting in a Chicago gangster movie. Juan moves closer and puts his arm around me, and I inch my way closer to him, I'm grateful for the ray of warmth on my back.

'Get away from that bitch, this is not a public relations office,' shouts a male voice from within blackness. Juan obeys and his body recoils.

Questions without answers race through my mind. What happened? Why are we here? Half an hour ago I was on my way to work at the *Instituto de Traductores y Interpretes* in Rio Rhin, strolling down Reforma Avenue with Juan and Emilia who had decided to accompany me because we enjoyed each other's company and they had nothing better to do. We laughed over something trivial and I felt the sun's warmth on my face.

Suddenly a battered Volkswagen Beetle sidled up and three young men dressed as students in their daggy jeans and t-shirts jumped out and walked towards us.

I thought they were Juan's friends. One asked Juan a question and another came towards me as though to shake my hand. Both were carrying rolled-up newspapers which unbeknownst to us concealed pistols. The one closet to me jabbed the gun, still wrapped in newspaper into my ribs and we were shoved into the Beetle. It was useless for us to protest or try to resist. We had been 'picked up' *(levantados)* as they say in Mexico.

So now I'm here in this place, a shabby and cavernous waiting room with no light, who knows where, who knows why. My thoughts race and collide, one bumping off another like moths attracted to a light bulb. I start to panic. I picture my mother. She'll never find me here; she doesn't speak Spanish and knows nothing about Mexico. If I don't know why I'm here and can't fathom what's happening, it will be impossible for her.

Mum had always questioned my decision to return to Mexico. She never understood. If all the world, according to her – including many Mexicans – wanted to emigrate to Australia, 'the land of milk and honey', why was I going in reverse? 'But Mum,' I answer as I try to explain, in my imaginary conversation, '...there are many Mexicans who are good people, generous and loving, others who are giving their lives in an attempt to change this world for the better'. At this moment these explanations ring hollow and don't even convince me one bit.

Mum lamented to anybody who would lend an ear that I, her daughter, had returned to Mexico to stay. Even after the birth of my two sons, she would speculate that Juan had kidnapped me for the white slave trade. Mrs Reece, a neighbour had put that idea into her head. She had read of such cases in the *Australian Women's Weekly*. Absurd as it was, I understood that this self-deception (I couldn't believe she really believed it) was some type of coping strategy for her. She saw my absence as a rejection of Australia and a betrayal of her, of all that she had given me with such devotion, sacrifice and pride. The white slave trade explanation was less painful. She would say, with almost a total lack of conviction, 'if you're happy, I'm happy'. I could never assure her that I was happy. There is no equivalent word in Spanish or English of orphan, for those mothers and fathers abandoned by their children.[1]

---

[1] This observation is drawn from the writings of Javier Marias.

Two agents are making a bee line towards Juan, they pull him up and walk him towards a doorway. When his body goes lank one of them shoulders him upright while the other kicks his legs from behind. They push and pull him forward. He turns his head and looks at me, his face stamped with a tattoo of terror. I strain forward to try and see him up closer but one of the men, almost reading my thoughts, grabs Juan's neck and pushes his head down to his chest. It occurs to me that maybe I'll never see him again. What if he disappears along with so many other Mexicans?

'We'll meet up in Tahiti,' I shout out to him. My captors had threatened to deport me from Mexico and I thought how complicated it would be for Juan, born in Mexico but with a Chinese father, to get a visa to Australia. Tahiti, an island I had visited, seemed a neutral solution, a peaceful paradise in the Pacific, floating half way between Mexico and Australia.

They take him away and I stay sitting on the edge of the concrete bench, next to an unknown Mexican woman and *la negra Emilia* I don't feel the cold anymore, my body and mind are numb.

A voice from inside the blackness, rings out.

'Throw me the blondie *(la güerita)*, over here.'

'No *compadre* she's not worth it, you know white meat is not juicy, no flavour, home grown products are better value,' another voice answers.

The three of us stiffen. Yes, I had understood correctly, their faces confirm I was right, the agent was insinuating that he would like to rape one of us. I was grateful, and offended at the same time to have been labelled as flavourless. Will they rape the Mexican woman or my friend Emilia whose blackness made her have more flavour? I pull my mini skirt over my knees.

My anguish turns to rage which leads me to shout out into the dark like the madwoman on Central Station in Sydney. 'I want to speak to my ambassador,' I repeat a little louder, 'I want to speak to my ambassador,' I wait, a little shocked at the depth of my anger, then I scream 'I WANT TO SPEAK TO MY AMBASSADOR.'

'Yes, yes you crazy blondie, soon you'll see your f_ _cking ambassador,' one of the agents answers, the others snort and belly laugh at what they knew would be his unkept promise.

Now used to the darkness, I see a queue of people, lined up against the wall waiting to hand in their daily reports to the *Comandante* seated at his desk to my right. They file past, ice-cream vendors, city garbage collectors wearing orange uniforms, women holding their empty tortilla baskets over their arms, all of them disguised undercover agents, just like the students who had kidnapped us on Reforma. I reprimand myself for my ignorance and naivety. I've been living in Mexico for over three years and working on an ad hoc committee of Amnesty International in London, for Mexican political prisoners. How could I have been so blind? Am I one of those ignorant bourgeois do-gooders who run around the world adopting other people's revolutions because they can't bring about their own? Why am I so unfamiliar with the way these secret agents operate? This is unexplored territory for me, a Mexico not mentioned in 'Unknown Mexico' (*México Desconocido*), a travel magazine I read frequently in anticipation of trekking around the country.

'I WANT TO SPEAK TO MY AMBASSADOR,' I scream for the fourth time.

'Now, I've had it, I'm sick of you,' says the balloon-cheeked agent, he pulls me up and drags me to a doorway, the same one that swallowed Juan.

'Downstairs you'll find your f_ _ ing ambassador,' he says as he kicks open the door to reveal a staircase going down.

He steps aside and indicates that I should descend. I move slowly and reluctantly, with every step I take an unknown creature is gnawing open a wide gaping cavern inside me and another is pouring lead into my legs. Although cold and scared, at least I had been at street level where the sounds of normal living, car horns, people shouting had seeped through, but now, where are they taking me? An underground tunnel? The antechamber to hell? Down there, in the bowels of the earth, nobody and least of all my ambassador, will ever find me. Although the darkness devours me once again, hope dies last, and I naively believe that the protector of Australian citizens will look for me.

For many years after my detention and release, I had a recurring dream that I was in a free-falling elevator going down, down, when it stopped, doors opened and I would step out into a black void. Without warning, a man grabbed me from behind. I would wake sweating and suffocating. My recurring nightmare turned out to have substance. The 1985 earthquake that shook Mexico City also revealed clandestine jails. In the rubble of the General Procurator of Justice (*Procaduría General de Justicia del Distrito Federal – PGDF*) were found 'cadavers in the trunks of cars, bound and gagged with marks of torture; these discoveries were never explained'.[2] Years later Juan would point out that we had been interrogated, four floors below ground level in the basement, of one of these clandestine jails in Tlaxcoaque, Mexico City.

Below, the interrogation began. But they don't interrogate, with confidence and arrogance they affirm you did such and such, then wait for the answer. The absurd accusations have no limit; they fire them at you one after another.

'You studied in the Patrice Lumumba University in Moscow,' (I had heard of Patrice Lumumba but he was African, not Russian, no?).

'You're a Russian spy,' (in spite of my not knowing a word of Russian, I could barely make myself understood in Spanish).

'You're donating money to subversive women's groups,' (this one even caused me to laugh inside. If these idiots only knew my Mexican feminist friends, San Angel ladies who lunch, who had so little in common with their more orthodox Australian and English counterparts).

At first, indignant, I answer, 'That's not true!' But after hours of repeated accusations coupled with hunger and sleep deprivation, I keep silent and don't even attempt to answer, which they interpret as a 'yes'. I am transformed from the accused to witness; I sit in a trance, silently waiting and watching. All this is not really happening.

---

[2] *La Jornada*, 19 de septiembre de 2015, Editorial, 'Sismos 30 años', p. 2.

For weeks afterwards I walked around in a fog which would abruptly lift when strangers mostly men, would bump into me and say, 'hello Jenny', as though we were old acquaintances. Then l realised that I was being followed.

After 72 hours we were released with a threat cloaked in an apology. Cynically, Nazar Haro, our interrogator,[3] said he really was on our side and a partisan to our cause but he advised us to keep away from the workers, and not to look to them as allies. If we did, he continued, he would have no option but to detain us and who knows if we would be so lucky as to be released again.

'You students are in the university, in the south of the city, stay there,' he said. 'The workers are in the north, in the factories, there's no reason for your paths to cross, but if you insist on looking for them', he continued, 'I'll find you, and you'll have to suffer the consequences'. I thought I hadn't understood properly, my Spanish was still faulty, what workers was he talking about? I knew no workers in Mexico. Everything about him – the smirk on his face, the mockery of our cause – spoke of contempt for us. He turned and marched out with his body guards scuttling behind him.

I stayed still for what seemed a long time, trying to fathom why this apparent and sudden about face. Juan jerked his head, 'let's go'. I felt scared to move, frightened that it was a trick and we'd be picked up again. Better the devil you know (than the devil you don't), my mum would say.

---

[3] Miguel Nazar Haro has been described as the number one torturer in Mexico and the head of the White Brigade that led the 'dirty war' against the young survivors of the '68 student movement. In 1982, this same character was involved in a crime of car theft worth $US30 million dollars; cars were stolen from Southern California in the United States and then sold over the border in Mexico. Later, he was accused as of being the protector of drug lords, but the CIA intervened so that he would not be prosecuted because he was one of its most important sources of information in Mexico. Rafael Rodríguez Castañeda, 'Nassar, importante, pero sólo pieza en la vieja sociedad DFS-CIA' (*Proceso*, núm. 284, 12-IV-82, p. 6, http://www.rebelion.org/noticia.php?id=144199; consulted: 20 September 2015).

When we arrived home to our flat we found it turned upside-down, papers strewn everywhere. On the kitchen floor were pages torn and scattered from the *Australian Woman's Cook Book* my aunt had given me, broken ceramic figurines smashed to pieces, my rings and a tape recorder missing. Magicians, without forcing the locks, they had passed through the front door and delved around in the intimacy of our bedroom. There they found my passport, where all the countries I had visited over the previous three years were registered. My turbulent life stamped and condensed in four pages. I had travelled via Central America, by bus, from Panama to Mexico, after disembarking from the ship, the Fair Star, which had crossed the Pacific Ocean from Sydney. And yes, I had also been in Moscow, a stamp in my passport proved it.

In the 1960s to travel by boat to visit the mother country, England, was fairly common, almost a rite of passage for some women of my generation and ilk. Using London as a base camp we'd work a while, save some and then take off to explore some part of Europe. Airline fares were so expensive compared to boat travel and we'd come so far, so we would adopt this nomadic existence, until we found ourselves, or thought we had, and return home to Australia, to settle down. This I never did manage.

Mexican secret police were not familiar with this bizarre behaviour of young Australians and above all of young women, which led them to deduce that only a Russian spy (me in this case) could have travelled so far for so long, and to so many places.

An explanation for accusing me of funding subversive feminist groups also surfaced: they had found in my house a list in my handwriting, of women's names, with an amount of money beside each name in a separate column. I was in charge of keeping a record of the contribution that each one paid to buy tea and coffee when our consciousness raising group met. Most bizarre and suspicious behaviour in their books.

However hard I tried, I could not explain to my interrogators what was the purpose of a feminist conscious raising group. They translated three pesos as three hundred dollars and so on, concluding that I had been subsidising Mexican women's groups to sit around and share their woes, but one of the worldlier agents said this was just a ruse, we were really speaking in some code with the purpose of organising a revolution like that raging in Nicaragua. He was right in the sense that our meetings were often serious affairs, we didn't consider them to be group therapy like our sisters in California did, but rather a valid form of feminist political action. Another agent commented that maybe it was some kind of women-only orgy.' These *gringas*' – Australians and Americans were all the same to him – 'are all whores', he said with authority.

My detention left me ambivalent about my identity as a Mexican. Jenny does not translate as Juanita. Juan accuses me to this day of living with a foot in each stirrup, as if I were riding on horseback, with a leg in each country, ready to take off any moment. To contemplate those what-if moments in one's life is a futile exercise, which my friends with Buddhist leanings abhor. They point out how unhealthy it is, all we have is the present they say, this raking over the past will lead you to a permanent wistful state, but I enjoy contemplating the roads not travelled, and have come to the age of the hyperfactual, the what-ifs of my life. What if I had been deported? What if I never left Australia? I confess there was a moment during the interrogations when, on hearing the screams of other women being tortured in adjacent cells, I pleaded in silence 'please, please deport me, now'.

Forty years on, I'm still living in the vibrant, complex City of Mexico and continue to be Juan's *compañera*. Nonetheless, once again violence and political repression,[4] has surfaced, threatening to suffocate, along with the smog, all who live here. I would never like to relive the hours of my detention, but I was lucky compared to the thousands of

---

[4] I first wrote this in September 2014, when 43 students from the Ayotzinapa Rural School were forcibly disappeared. The case is one of the most emblematic episodes of violation of human rights in the recent history of Mexico. In 2020, their relatives are still looking for them.

people who have disappeared in Mexico in the last ten years. The 43 students of Ayotizinapa and those other bodies found in clandestine graves have no chance of calling out for their ambassador.

One of my sons, now forty-odd has just finished reading this narrative, he looks at me perplexed.

'What you have written scares me,' he says almost whispering, but then he starts firing the questions.

'Mum, were you and Dad really that innocent?'

'Don't kid me, did they really kidnap you and Dad just because they felt like it?'

He doesn't give me a chance to answer, 'Dad was a Maoist, wasn't he?'

I didn't try to answer immediately, I could tell he was upset and not in a listening mode.

'You wanted to overthrow the system. Did you think they were going to sit back and let you go ahead?'

Once again, I attempt to explain to him our story, of how and why I came to Mexico, how I met Juan. Of the utopian vision we had along with others involved in the 1968 student movement, the brutal repression his father and I had witnessed. My participation in Amnesty International. He has heard it all before in bits and pieces but now he is exasperated.

'Mum you tend to ramble,' he says, 'you have so many versions of how you came to Mexico and why you stayed, which one is true?'

'One thing is why I came and another why I stayed,' I say. He's not satisfied, it's getting too complicated.

'You were in love with my Dad and you wanted children, keep it simple,' he says.

My narrative has made him anxious, especially since he has decided to leave Mexico and live elsewhere. He says he doesn't want his children to grow up here, always looking over their shoulder in fear, living and dying in the extremes.

I try to explain to him that all the versions he has heard from me are true, it just depends on whom I am talking to. He shakes his head, opens the door and leaves.

Journeys

Learning in Mexico

Raewyn Connell

RAEWYN CONNELL'S Twitter ID reads: Busy sociologist, obscure poet, hard-line feminist, dangerous lefty, what's not to love? It's almost true. She has researched questions of gender, class, education, and global patterns in knowledge. Her work has been translated into 19 languages, including Spanish and Portuguese. She has now retired from an academic career and begun life as an agitator; an early result is her 2019 book *The Good University*. Raewyn has been active in the labour movement, the peace movement and work for gender equality. Her website can be found at: www.raewynconnell.net. She is also on Twitter @raewynconnell.net.

I haven't lived in Mexico. I have visited multiple times, for different reasons. I love the country and its people and have tried to learn about them. This has taken 49 years so far.

I don't have conversational Spanish though I can read texts in a rough way. I've hoped to build a certain kind of South-South connection, and perhaps my stories show some possibilities, and some difficulties, in this project.

THE TEMPLE

My first visit was 49 years ago, when I was spending a year as an unpaid post-doctoral hanger-on in the famous sociology department at the University of Chicago. My partner Pam supported us by working as a visa officer at the British consulate, where she became an expert on the post-imperial hypocrisies of the UK Nationality Act. Nixon was in power, the US invasion of Cambodia and the Kent State killings happened that year, and we marched on Washington by Volkswagen. (The massacre in Tlatelolco square had happened just two years before, but that hadn't registered in Australian media.) When the university closed in summer, Pam took leave and we went for a month to have a quiet explore in Mexico.

Pam had some conversational Spanish, from time in Nicaragua as a child. We were tourists, but tourists with a focus: archaeology. I had studied history at university and visited some Mycenaean sites in Greece, so I thought myself almost a professional. Pam was tolerant of this folly. We went by crowded bus to Teotihuacán and, after a hot and dusty day, knew that this was a bigger story than Mycenae. We walked to the National Museum of Anthropology and gazed respectfully at the giant Olmec head and the colourful ears of shrivelled prehistoric maize.

As a student I had read, in a creaky translation, Bernal Díaz del Castillo's narrative of the appalling events of 1519-1521, so I knew a little about Tenochtitlán. But there wasn't even a decent ruin left, the Spaniards had seen to that. For the archaeological enthusiast there was only one direction to go: east. We went by train to Mérida and spent the next few days going by local buses over the dry scrubland to ChichenItzá, Dzibilchaltún and Uxmal. The country felt a bit like the Mallee or the Hay plain – we wouldn't have been surprised if a few emus had wandered past.

Those sites were splendid and shiver-making, but they were Postclassic. That was not good enough. The displays at the National Museum had sold us on the Classic. Label on a small Maya statue there: 'Illustrious personage wearing rich apparel' – who could resist it?

So to Palenque we went. The helpful folk in Mérida had recommended a hotel near the station, modest but very new. Indeed, the building work was not exactly finished, but we were young and in love, and finding our way, and it was all good. At the site of the ancient city there was almost no-one around, we had the place practically to ourselves.

If the bush in northern Yucatán had felt familiar, this absolutely did not. Dense forest up the hillsides, the trees a solid, brilliant green, the air damp, it felt as if a powerful vegetable world was just being held at bay. And there lived this cluster of deep grey structures, some of them artificial hills in their own right. There had been some restoration, but it wasn't obtrusive.

We climbed up the steep stairs of the Temple of the Inscriptions, the most elegant pyramid I know, sat in the shade, and drank in the site from there. In that situation I play mind games, populating the buildings with a few hundred people – no, a few thousand – no, tens of thousands. Palenque wasn't Tikal or Calakmul, but in the period these buildings date from, it was a rich city. And the gorgeous artwork, the glyphs and the relief sculptures of gods and goddesses: imagine the labour, the sheer organization involved. And then flip back to these stones standing in the strong sun, deep grey above a green hollow, with no voices sounding.

At that time, we couldn't visit the crypt of the Temple of the Inscriptions. So, I didn't take much notice of the fine details in the *Guide Bleu*. Much later, after Pam had died, I read a book about the decipherment of the Maya glyphs and learnt what we hadn't seen.

We had been sitting on top of a tomb. The whole thing was a bloody great funerary monument. Less than twenty years before, a real archaeologist, a very patient man, had dug down for several years and found the astonishing burial of the king who had ruled at the height of the city's power. Like other cities in the region, and contrary to the old image of the classic Maya as peaceful philosophers measuring the slow passage of time, Palenque was ruled by a dynasty frequently at war, embroiled in power politics along the Usumacinta valley. On later visits to Mexico it was sobering to think how much I had missed, the first time around.

WE HAVE WITH US TODAY...

Fast forward thirty years, please. Lights? Camera rolling? It's Y2K, I'm in my fifties, widowed, a sole parent, based in Australia again after a short unhappy stint in the global North, and well on in an academic career. I'm regarded as an expert on certain topics, especially the new field of social research on masculinities. This gets me invitations to conferences and universities, and the field has become international. Recently I've given lectures in countries ranging from Latvia to Chile. Now an invitation comes from Mexico.

It was the start of a different kind of engagement. I made five and a half visits over the next fourteen years, giving lectures and seminars, holding meetings and doing interviews. Two of my books were published in Mexico, I wrote some articles for Mexican publications, and appeared once or twice in mass media.

The five visits each lasted a week or so, apart from one cut short when my mother went into hospital and the family called me home. The half was a seminar done electronically, not by Skype but by a superior conferencing system known to the colleagues in Tijuana. The visits in the flesh took me at different times to Morelos, Cuernavaca, Juárez and Guadalajara, and to the Distrito Federal (DF) on every visit.

The first invitation came from colleagues at the university-wide Gender Studies programme at UNAM, one of the largest feminist academic programmes in the world, perhaps the largest. They wanted to explore the new research about masculinities. There was already a Mexican literature about this, going back to Octavio Paz at least. In the 1990s a gender-conscious activism had developed among a network of Mexican men. So I wasn't bringing a revelation, but my visit did provide a focus for theoretical discussion and critique. The debate lasted through four days of seminars and lectures. I've rarely been so well interrogated!

I learnt about the importance of psychoanalytic thought for Mexican feminism, at least for its academic wing. Through several visits

I learnt about the practical agendas too. I remember a discussion in Guadalajara about the shape of Mexican feminism, which emphasised that the number-one struggle was about violence; next, health and education. Some colleagues from UNAM were wary of the new attention being given to men and masculinity; there was a concern about men taking over territory that women had opened up. I met some men in the network who had thought about this issue carefully, and conceived their work as a parallel, supportive struggle. But I think there were others who did not care about links with feminism.

In the university world I was mostly in a privileged environment. Some of it very privileged, such as the elegant country retreat of a couple who must have been on the fringe of the ruling class. But I wasn't entirely in a bubble. In DF, I took note of the northern district, which I remembered as shanty-town country in 1970, now a vast tract of concrete-block construction, still crowded and bare. As a socialist I was thrilled to give a public lecture in the Auditorio Salvador Allende in Guadalajara.

On two of these visits I travelled with my daughter Kylie. The first was when she was a teenager. Friends showed her around while I was doing seminars and talks, introducing her to young people who took her under their wing. I was immensely grateful to all involved. I was still scared. As well as normal parental terror, there was a question of language, as Kylie did not speak much Spanish then. Waiting till 3 a.m. for her to come back from a night listening to bands with her new friends was not one of my high points. But that night was a good one for her.

Ten years later it was a matter of her taking care of me. She now spoke Spanish fluently, had worked in South America, and was streetwise on three continents. I realised, as she navigated back to the metro one evening from a successful book-shopping expedition and dinner out in DF, that I was a liability in terms of safety at night. She knew what to do, I didn't.

There was another side to this change. Between these visits, I had undertaken gender transition, or as some trans women call it, gender affirmation. During the earlier visits I had been living as a man. Perhaps some people thought it odd that I never joined men's groups, but most took my gender category for granted. Now I was travelling officially as a woman.

I won't bore you with the back-story, but I now had to reckon with the consequences. Though attitudes have been changing, some Anglophone feminists are extremely hostile to transsexual women. In certain parts of the world there are socially recognised gender-changing groups: the *kathoey* of Thailand for instance. In other places, trans groups are regarded as disgusting, an offence to religion and morality, and are targets of violence. I knew this was the situation in some Mexican contexts, and I didn't know what response I could expect.

In fact, the feminists who next invited me to Mexico were wonderfully supportive. They clearly thought I had something to offer: organised a workshop on research methods and a public lecture on decolonising gender, introduced me to movement activists, and took me to an exhibition of women's art. They did want to discuss transgender issues, and took seriously the account I gave... At the end of the visit the colleagues made me a gift of beautiful earrings and embroidered blouses. I think I am allowed to cry.

MAKE STRAIGHT IN THE DESERT A HIGHWAY

I learned in a different way from a short visit to Cd. Juárez, during a campaign about violence against women. The background is well known. Around 1990 the battered bodies of women and girls were being found on vacant lots and in the desert near the city. Many had been abducted, then raped, tortured, and their bodies dumped. As years passed the numbers mounted into the hundreds. There was almost complete impunity for the men who did the killings.

In 1993 a retired accountant, Ester Chávez, decided she had read too many news reports about dead women. She made herself unpopular by keeping the news clippings, challenging police and officials, comforting victims' families, and leading street marches. In 2001 the mother of one of the murdered girls set up a group called *Nuestras Hijas de Regreso a Casa* (Our Daughters to Return Home). Mexican feminists increasingly spoke of *feminicidio*, women being killed simply because they were women. A movie was made about the issue, *El Traspatio*, and a well-known Mexican playwright, Humberto Robles, wrote a powerful theatre piece called *Mujeres de Arena*. Meanwhile the killings continued, now targeting protestors too. This reached a vile climax in 2010 when the mother of a murdered girl, protesting outside the governor's office, was chased and shot dead by an assassin. The event was captured on CCTV: I have seen the video. About the same time a group of artists in DF, called for an international solidarity campaign.

An Australian group formed in response to this call, taking the name Sydney Action for Juárez (SAFJ). We were active for several years, compiling information, feeding it to Australian media, speaking at demonstrations and meetings, raising money for women's groups in Juárez, mounting performances of *Mujeres de Arena*, writing for online sites, and more. We found it difficult to make direct contact, but a new opportunity came in 2013. A conference was planned at the *Colegio de la Frontera Norte* about 'Men and the Politics of Violence', the annual meeting of the progressive Mexican men's studies association, AMEGH for its initials in Spanish. I had met some of its members on earlier visits, and I was invited to give the keynote address. I travelled there with Rosarela Meza, one of the SAFJ organisers.

The city reminded me of Broken Hill, though it has a population bigger than Adelaide. We flew in over desert. The immediate area is scrubby, arid and flat, with bare mountains in the background. There is money here: from the aeroplane you can see larger houses with swimming pools. There is a university, a school system and hospitals, with a middle class of managers, technicians, teachers and nurses, and government office staff. Some of the money flows to the factory and transport workers, but it's far from a workers' paradise. Most of the people are poor, many are recent arrivals from rural areas further south. The urban sprawl is small houses closely packed. There hasn't been much public investment.

It was called El Paso del Norte by the Spaniards, and became a border post after the United States grabbed the northern half of Mexico in the 1840s. In the 1880s it was renamed Ciudad Juárez after the leader of resistance against the French invasion. It played a role in the revolution – Pancho Villa was based in the area, the town was fought over and became a military base. It was one of the main conduits of US/Mexico trade throughout the 20th century, and there is now tremendous truck traffic up and down the highway. In the neoliberal era, Juárez became a site of low-wage manufacturing for export and grew very fast. There are said to be 400 factories here: from the air you can see swathes of them, all surrounded by big trucks.

That's the background of femicide. A vulnerable workforce of migrant women, with little social support or unionisation or community protection. The main sources of wealth are male-dominated and unstable – *maquilas*, long-distance transport and *narcotráfico*. There are several paramilitary forces in the city, including the state police, the federal police, and the drug cartels themselves, which are basically private armies recruited from unemployed young men, fighting to control the flow of cocaine and marijuana into the world's richest market, the USA. Then there is the border, which was militarised long before Donald Trump: the constant presence of an armed barrier across the land must add some craziness to the local scene.

On our first day in the city we were met by Itzel from the *Red Mesa de Mujeres*, the coalition of women's groups in the city, who took us immediately to a meeting at their office. They had rescheduled from morning to afternoon in order to meet us. Nine women from different groups, plus the office staff. We talked together for a couple of hours, starting a bit stiffly as they must have been wondering who the hell we were, but warming up markedly and ending with lots of goodwill and photographs.

Then we were taken to visit the *Casa Amiga* named for Ester Chávez (she had died in 2009). This was the new women's support centre, located in one of the working-class districts, providing medical, legal, counselling and child care services, and safety. We met the director Irma, who showed us over the centre and discussed its work. We finished with a companionable meal with the staff in their back room, and a photo-op out the front.

They struck me as a very practical, no-nonsense group. They calmly described the intimidation they had weathered. Threats from angry men go with women's activism everywhere, but with lots of illegal weapons around here, the threats could easily turn lethal. The *Casa Amiga* group seemed to have solid community connections, providing services that were badly needed, for children and men as well as for adult women.

On our third day we met again with the women from the *Mesa*, this time focussing on practical issues and what kind of support could usefully be given from a distance. Women's groups in the city, it seemed, had recently become more organised on an NGO model. The two centres must cost a fair amount to run, including staff salaries. Irma mentioned that the building for *Casa Amiga* was donated by a private funder.

The conference on men and the politics of violence was small and focussed. The organisers had built a Day of the Dead altar near the entrance, with a sign mentioning 9,500 killings (men as well as women) in the region in the last five years. I gave the keynote address on the opening day; it was translated sentence by sentence, everyone concentrated hard and it went well. It was published later in the book of the conference. That evening I ran a workshop on research methods for studies of masculinity. There was very enthusiastic involvement and at the end we could hardly make the discussion groups stop, almost needing to switch off the lights.

The academic part of the visit was straightforward: I knew the ropes. What wasn't familiar was the stuff happening outside. The only open sign of the violence that Rosarela and I saw was a truckload of *Policía Federal*, in black like some commando detachment, driving along a main road with their sub-machine guns and helmets ready. We were told that most of the *Policía Federal* had been withdrawn from the city and the rate of killings had gone down.

I don't mind admitting that I was scared shitless. If our meetings had attracted hostile attention I wouldn't have known what to do. The Mexican state had no particular reason to protect me or Rosarela, foreign agitators up to no good in the USA's *traspatio* (backyard). In fact we were very carefully looked after by the conference organisers and the feminist comrades. I hope our experiment in solidarity was worthwhile for them.

I came away with enormous respect for the activists living in Juárez, and new understanding of what they were facing. Femicide and homophobic violence here don't grow out of traditional machismo, because Juárez isn't a traditional community. It's a profoundly modern city, transformed by the market agenda and the international economy. Femicide is a brutal assertion of male dominance, true. But it's a new patriarchy being built, not just an old one reproduced. And if that's right, the Juárez story is even more alarming, because this kind of violence won't be fading away when old patriarchal traditions die. Many of these conditions exist in other parts of the world. *De te fabula narratur*.

AT THE END...

Perhaps Mexican archaeology wasn't a bad place to start but it wasn't the place to end. In the course of these trips I learnt about a modern society in jagged, disruptive change. I learnt about a many-sided women's movement with a trajectory and culture seriously different from those I knew. I went to research centres and bookshops, wrote notes from the talks and seminars, did interviews, and met as many teachers and researchers as possible. So I learnt about an intellectual culture of depth and power, which is massively under-recognised in the Anglosphere and almost unknown in Australia.

And in the long run I discovered more than Mexico. These visits breathed life into a long-term project about feminist thought across the postcolonial world. This has led me to four other continents, not to mention a couple of oceans, and it's still going on. Learning in Mexico has been important for me in learning about the world.

On the track of the elusive B. Traven

Heidi Zogbaum

HEIDI ZOGBAUM, born in Germany and long-time resident of Melbourne, is now a lecturer and deputy-director of the Institute of Latin American Studies at La Trobe University in Melbourne. Her PhD was published as *B. Traven: A Vision of Mexico* in 1992 by Scholarly Resources of Wilmington/Delaware.

I arrived for the first time in Mexico in early January 1984 in order to finalise my PhD on the German-Mexican writer B. Traven for which I was enrolled at the Institute of Latin American Studies of La Trobe University in Melbourne. The signs of the recent financial collapse were everywhere and the $US350 which I brought with me, sustained me in moderate luxury for an amazingly long time. I was lucky because I already spoke fluent Spanish and had a ready-made network of contacts through a friend from Spain. They took me by the hand and introduced me to their extended families and their wonderful Sunday lunches, to Coyoacán, Teotihuacán, Xochimilco, Cuernavaca, Puebla and to everything Mexicans have to give by ways of warmth, friendship, generosity and acceptance. I needed that because living in Mexico City was precarious and, coming from Melbourne, I was not used to it.

Trouble started early, in fact upon arrival late at night. My Spanish friend had booked a room at the Maria Isabel Sheraton through his company at a special discount rate. But the receptionist informed me that there was no reservation and that I would have to pay the rack rate. I was aware that this is the oldest trick of receptionists to pocket the price difference but before the era of mobile phones and no hotel director on duty, there was little I could do. The next morning the famous Mexico City smog was clearly visible from my window. Shortly afterwards, with the help of friends, I found a very nice room in Calle Río Tigris, just a stone's throw away from Reforma. I was all set to begin to unravel the mysteries of B. Traven.

His home where he lived out his life, was in Calle Rio Mississippi in walking distance. I made an appointment with his widow, Rosa Elena Luján, who received me gracefully. In a small way, this wonderfully comfortable low-slung house, by then surrounded by eight-story apartment blocks, became a second home. We shared many coffees, meals and laughs. But nobody was allowed free access to Traven's archive because the widow did not actually understand what was in it. Most documentation was in German. Every time I came, I was only given one or two folders with documents and sometimes I was asked to translate something for her from German to English or Spanish.

It dawned on me that this narcissistic and self-centred man had left his young widow in an unenviable situation: she was made the guardian of the 'secret of his identity' which meanwhile had ceased to be much of a secret. She had to learn from a German scholar who her late husband actually was. He had pieced together that the man known as B. Traven, the author of a string of world famous books published before the Second World War, had once been the editor of a small anarchist newspaper in Munich by the name of Ret Marut. Traven had never confided in her but strung her along with his stories about being in constant danger of discovery. That danger had long since disappeared in 1926 in a general amnesty for all political prisoners, which not only included the few survivors of the Munich Soviet Republic of 1919 of which Ret Marut was one, but also Adolf Hitler. But Traven's 'secret' was too good a business ploy to give up because it helped him stay in the public eye which was no longer interested in anarchist world views or anything else smacking of the extreme Left. Eventually, the 'secret' came to define his personality.

Nor did the widow know details about his life before she met him on the film set of *The Treasure of the Sierra Madre* in 1948. This job fell to me, to cover the period since 1921 when he arrived in Mexico and compare what he presented as 'documentary accounts' in his books to what actually happened. It turned out that Traven was less than honest most of the time but very keen to present himself as a swashbuckling hero. While attributing to himself a most wondrously adventurous life, he lived quietly on a farm in Tamaulipas. The stories he retold in some of his early books were lived by others who had told them to this 'American' with a distinct German accent who was such a patient listener. And when he did not vicariously live through great adventures, he misunderstood much of what was around him. It is not surprising that I never received a thank-you note from Sra Luján after I sent her my finished book in 1992. I had just turned into another embarrassment for her, knowing more about her husband than she did, and not all very nice. It was poor repayment for her kindness and I wish that it could have been otherwise.

In those days it was well understood – except by me – that being robbed in Mexico City was the equivalent of an initiation. In a restaurant in the Zona Rosa, I hung my handbag on the back of my chair and when it came to paying the bill, there was no handbag. The owner was embarrassed and could not get rid of me quickly enough, even without paying. Since I had travel insurance, I needed a police certificate. So, I checked up the nearest police station and went there. It was an evil place and scenes of remarkable brutality happened before my eyes. Nobody paid attention to me until the doctor of the attached gaol waved me into his surgery. In a very graceful Mexican way, he made clear to me that I should leave as soon as possible. I took his advice. At night, I saw a German friend who was horrified that I should have walked into a Mexican police station. She assured me that I was lucky to have come out in one piece. I began to appreciate the friendly Mexican doctor more than ever. But that did not give me the desired police certificate.

Again, through friends and *enchufes*, I was able to make an appointment at the local administration of the Cuauhtémoc neighbourhood. The cousin of a cousin introduced me to his colleague in charge of police matters and the two exchanged niceties and flatteries and addressed each other incessantly as *'licenciado, por favor'* and *'licenciado, gracias'* and *'licenciado... licenciado'*. I had never heard such a performance because undergraduate degrees were becoming the norm in Australia. I was seated in a waiting room and the initial *licenciado* disappeared, having performed his favour to a distant relative. And there I sat. An American couple arrived who had been robbed in an underground station. They waited for about an hour and then gave up. More people came and went and I still sat there. The *licenciado* in charge dealt with people much lower down in the queue but not with me. I finally made inquiries from a few office girls who could not or would not answer my question, but invited me to share some cake with them. So, we sat in a round, gossiped and giggled, when the *licenciado* walked by. He just looked at us and quickly asked me into his room. I explained my problem and the paperwork was speedily dealt with. I was free to go home. The poor *licenciado*, whose clientele would include more and more foreign tourists due to the rapidly rising petty-crime rate in the city, was afraid of having to admit that he was not up to dealing with foreigners because he had no English. Once he realised that I knew sufficient Spanish, he was perfectly amenable. Since then I never hang my handbag on the back of my chair.

This was not the last time I was robbed. I had another bag cut open with a razor blade in a bus going down Reforma. Many people must have seen it, but nobody warned me for reasons which were later explained to me. Who wants to make the acquaintance of a razor blade? But by that time, I was smarter. I had nothing of value in the bag and always carried my worldly goods in a clear plastic folder for all the world to see. The little money I needed was in my jeans pocket. I had become robbery-proof and remained so until my departure a few months later.

When walking back from the metro station to my abode I watched with dismay as more and more apartment blocks rose up where once beautiful villas in a Spanish colonial style, as it was called, had stood in immaculate gardens. The way they were built seemed extremely ramshackle: a few slim pillars holding up a concrete slab, piled up seven or eight times. The sides were filled in with a single layer of bricks and the fronts consisted of aluminium frames with large glass panes inserted. I always tried to walk in the middle of the street, expecting that with the slightest earth tremor, the glass panes would be loosened and come sailing down into the street with deadly effect. I was spared the experience. The next big earthquake came the following year.

Since B. Traven made his name mostly writing about the south of Mexico, Chiapas and Tabasco, I had to follow in his tracks. I took the bus from Mexico City via Veracruz to Villahermosa in Tabasco, retracing in reverse the steps of Hernán Cortes. I had friends there who I knew from Spain. It was a very different world and to my understanding, I had moved closer to the 'real' Mexico of small towns, of hammocks, of maize farmers, of fishermen – but also of oilmen. Where I lived in the capital, I could always see the PEMEX tower, which, I was told, was home to quite a number of 'dynasties', where father bequeathed his job to his son, regardless of qualifications. It was the navel in a universe of corruption.

Through my friends, I fell in with a group of Frenchmen who were contracted to PEMEX in Villahermosa. Through them I understood the oil company's technological backwardness. Their job was to measure the pressure in drill shafts. Mexico, it seemed, was unable to train its own recruits and contracted very highly paid European engineers. In their company I witnessed my first murder. Stepping out of a restaurant, we saw a man run for his life, closely followed by a small truck with six men armed with semi-automatic guns. The victim had turned into a narrow lane and the truck could not follow. The six jumped down and also began to run. Then there was the report of several gunshots. I was informed that this was quite normal in Villahermosa and that most mornings somebody or other was discovered in a laneway. 'Just don't be stupid enough to go there and check on the man!' I was told.

One day we went to Palenque. It was a revelation, and not just because of the heat. The workmanship, the remaining stucco and colours, the reliefs of Maya royalty, the burial chambers, all spoke of greatness. The township of Palenque nearby, miserable, dusty, poverty-stricken, bore no resemblance to the ruins and only spoke of great loss.

And then part of the French/Spanish clique accompanied me to San Cristóbal de Las Casas. We came to call it San Cristóbal de La Laguna because of its uncanny resemblance to the old city of La Laguna in Tenerife in the Canary Islands. But then, Spanish colonial architecture was as standardised as the later British version which spread from India through Malaya all the way to Australia. Here was Indian territory with daily street markets, wonderful handicrafts and unlimited avenues to spend one's money. We made friends with a young Spanish hotel director who invited us to stay in his first-class hotel at half price so that the hotel would not look empty. Needless to say, we were all delighted. We went on excursions to the surrounding countryside, to Chamula and Zinacantán to gawk at Tzotzil and Tzeltal Indians who had been made famous by the books of B. Traven.

I also made the acquaintance of Gertrude Duby. I had never heard much good of her and my one and only personal contact confirmed this. But when her volume of black-and-white photographs of Lacandons came out, all was forgiven and forgotten. What a magnificent monument to a dying culture!

My principal task in Chiapas was to find out about the reality of the mahogany logging industry and compare it to Traven's descriptions in his so-called Jungle Novels. I could still find a few of the old loggers who had seen the primitive and cruel industry with their own eyes. I even found the descendants of people who had met the man who, in 1923, called himself Traven Torsvan, Norwegian photographer, with a huge camera which he had difficulty operating. There were many Germans in Chiapas in the old days and sometimes Traven dropped his pretences to the point where he actually talked in German to some of them. He must have felt very safe in this remote area.

His portrayal of the *monterías*, the logging camps, and the debt slavery which was practised there to maintain the workforce, was rarely exaggerated. Traven had found his topic which would keep him writing until the outbreak of the Second World War. After that he lost his dramatic flair and produced work quite unworthy of him. He relapsed into the style and content of writing of Ret Marut, the opinionated hack from Munich, who pretended to have knowledge of the world but betraying his limitations at every turn. He tried to dabble in archaeology and launch himself as a connoisseur of Indian art, of world affairs, and any other topic under the sun. It was pitiful. Mexico and the aftermath of the Revolution had made him into a writer. But the Mexico after 1945 no longer allowed scope for an anarcho-syndicalist world-view. Despite my intense dislike of the man, I felt pity for him. He just could not imagine a world that was not circling around him and his 'secret.'

Our hotel director friend did me one last favour and booked a room in a brand new hotel, just converted from an old monastery, in Oaxaca. Everything about Oaxaca was wonderful and returning to the bustle of Mexico City was like a nightmare. But that began to look quite different once I arrived in Los Angeles where I stayed for a while with Australian friends. Robberies in Mexico were generally carried out by people who had no other way of feeding their families or themselves. They did not hurt anyone as long as they were not frustrated in their purpose. They were no sadists who took pleasure in humiliating others or enjoying their pain. If I had to be robbed, let it be in Mexico! The insincerity of Californians also came as a shock. They seemed friendly and open but were really only looking for their own reflection in my eyes, or so I saw it. It was quite a new experience for which neither Mexico nor Australia had prepared me.

I returned once more to Mexico in 1998 to stay for the summer with my friend Ruth Adler. Very little of what was so prominent in

1984 was still there. Mexico had changed dramatically. It had become a more open and cosmopolitan country where US$350 did not stretch far. A knowledge of English was now everywhere, especially among the young. The *licenciado* in charge of street crime at Cuauhtémoc *ayuntamiento* had certainly been replaced with someone more able to deal with tourists. But the nature of crime in the capital had also gone upmarket. Robberies were no longer predominantly the small-scale pick-pocketing of individuals or small groups of desperate men. Violent house invasions had become common and certain once beautiful areas around Coyoacán looked deserted. My Mexican friends explained that the owners had moved North to the United States for safety. They lived in Pedregál and had a number of vicious dogs patrolling their property.

I suddenly became homesick for the Mexico I had known in 1984.

The posting

Ruth Adler

Between 1998 and 2000, I was posted as First Secretary and later Counsellor at the Australian Embassy in Mexico City. I had lived in Mexico as a student in the mid-1980s and I had always had the idea that I would like to go back there some time. Like so many decisions in my life, this one was serendipitous. I was on maternity leave when the postings list came out and, on a whim, sent-off my application for the First Secretary/Deputy Head of Mission role in Mexico City. Several months later on a Friday afternoon, while I was still on maternity leave, the phone rang. It was the director of the department's Staffing Operations Section. My daughter Amelia – who was less than a year old at that stage – was sitting on my hip and I had that Friday afternoon feeling of tiredness. He asked me how I was and then if I was sitting-down. Although I was not, I said I was and then he said that a postings list was about to come out.

'And your name's on it,' he said. 'You are going to Mexico City.'

'Really? What?'

'Congratulations, Ruth!'

I put down the receiver. My mind raced ahead several months. What had I done? Amelia would be just one when we left Australia and our son Jesse would be three by that time. How would I cope with two small children in Mexico City? What if it was hard to get a good nanny or carer?

'Oh my God! What I have I done?' I said aloud.

We were just about to move into a new house in Canberra and then, five months later, we would be packing-up again. What sort of madness was that? I had many sleepless nights over the coming months wondering how it was all going to work out.

That night I told my husband Conrad the moment he walked in the door that I had got the posting. He kissed me and said congratulations.

The next few months were a blur of pre-posting preparations. Compulsory pre-posting training in finance and security, and a consular course which included a visit to Goulburn gaol, just in case we were ever called upon to visit Australians in prison in our countries of accreditation. In my case, the embassy in Mexico City was also accredited to Cuba, El Salvador, Guatemala, Honduras and Nicaragua. While there were relatively few consular cases in those days in Mexico and Central America, those that were on the embassy books tended to have their own unique challenges and sensitivities.

My pre-posting preparations also involved a one-month intensive refresher course in Spanish and seemingly endless paperwork, including inventories of personal effects going to post, diplomatic passports for Conrad and I, ordinary passports for the children, and so on. As the plan was for Conrad to divide his time between Canberra and Mexico City, we had decisions to make about what to take and what to leave at home. Given that we had a relatively generous allowance in terms of what we could bring to post and were uncertain of the availability of some things, we stocked-up on Asian groceries, curries, spices, S-26 toddler milk formula and – believe it or not – Huggies nappies! Someone had told me that the quality of Huggies nappies in Mexico was not the same as in Australia and so I stocked-up! Then there was the quite enjoyable trip to Jim Murphy's where we purchased 11 cases of wine (the amount we were allowed as foreign diplomatic staff to bring in duty free) and some spirits. By the time, the 'uplift' day came, I was exhausted, but relieved and excited once the removalist's van pulled out of the driveway. With half of our stuff gone, our house looked minimalist and tidy, and I wished it looked that way all the time!

A few days later, we were on our way. We stayed overnight in Sydney en route to say goodbye to my parents and family there, and then flew from Sydney to Los Angeles on Qantas. With a one and a three old in tow, we were the family that no one wanted to be seated near in the business class compartment and we received a few stares over newspapers as we boarded and settled into our seats! With Amelia being so small, her business class seat was like a little cot for her and she slept much of the time, except for when she wanted to practise her recently found ability to walk, wanting to toddle up and down the aisle of the plane.

After a few days in Los Angeles and San Francisco, we were Mexico City-bound. We arrived in the afternoon and were met by a colleague from the embassy and transferred to Cuernavaca, where we did some Spanish language training for two weeks – an intensive refresher course for me and an introductory Spanish course for Conrad. The brief period of language training was almost like a holiday, with classes in the mornings and time for study and to explore Cuernavaca in the afternoons. Upon our return to Mexico City, we were installed in the Hotel Nikko in Polanco, not far from the embassy, where we were to stay until we found long-term accommodation. At first, we thought it was wonderful – we were in a junior suite, which seemed very luxurious to us, but then reality hit.

I started work at the embassy within a day or two of arriving and Conrad stayed at the hotel with the children. Each day, we would have breakfast, I would go to work and then he would need to work out ways to entertain the children for the day. The Hotel Nikko had an artificial electronic fish tank with a changing display of swimming fish and Conrad's morning routine would include a visit to the fish tank. He would park the children in front of the tank, while he read a newspaper or a book. The display would change every few minutes and the children would be transfixed by the colourful, ever-changing images of fish until – after about 15 minutes – they became restless and bored.

Over the road from the Nikko was a dusty children's playground and each day, after the fish tank, they would go to the park and the children would jump on the trampolines and be pushed on the swings. There was also a very tall, rickety slide and an old-fashioned rusty see-saw. There was one occasion when Jesse climbed the ladder of the slide and then got stuck at the top, because he was too afraid to come down from such a great height! The see-saw was also problematic, because it was not very stable and it was quite hard for the adult at the other end to manoeuvre it up and down! After the park, it would be time for lunch, an afternoon nap and cartoons dubbed in Spanish on the hotel cable TV! This was probably our children's first intensive exposure to Spanish.

After a few days, a Mexican woman by the name of Rosa called on us. Rosa had worked for my predecessor and was looking for a job. An older, kindly person, she did not seem enamoured of the idea of caring for small children, but she needed a job and we needed a carer. So, without hesitation, we engaged her and she came every day to help with the children and later, when we found permanent accommodation, she came to live with us. She was utterly reliable and I was very reliant on her, and I could not have done my job without her being there. Rosa spoke no English and so very quickly the children acquired Spanish.

One of the problems with being in a hotel was the lack of cooking and laundry facilities. Eating in the hotel, ordering room service and using the hotel laundry was expensive. With four of us, we always had a lot of washing and Rosa tried to help by handwashing the children's clothes, which would be draped throughout the room and the bathroom to dry. We desperately needed to find somewhere to live. The plan was that we would look for a place following our arrival. My predecessor had lived in a comfortable house in San Angel, an affluent neighbourhood in the southern part of Mexico City, but – for some reason – the embassy had decided to give up the lease on the property when he left. We started to look for a place from the day I arrived.

But, it was not easy. Mexican landlords sought to charge foreign embassy tenants exorbitant rents for houses and apartments which would have only fetched half the asking price in the local market. The embassy would not allow us to take some of the places I found and liked, because they were deemed to be too far away, the cost was just above the embassy's rent ceiling or the property in question had 'maintenance issues'. We spent many weeks searching for a place and ended-up moving to a serviced apartment, because it was getting too expensive to keep us in a hotel. We were in one serviced apartment for several weeks and then another. We had to move because the lease ran out on the first one and the owners would not renew it, which we suspected was because they did not like having a family with small children for an extended period of time. Meanwhile, the frustrating and tedious process of searching for suitable accommodation continued.

Our patience was, however, eventually rewarded when – after we had seen about 70 houses and apartments – the real estate agent who had been assisting us with the search told us that something she thought we might like had come onto the market. It was in the Colonia Condesa, a part of the city we had not considered and which, according to the agent, was not an area where 'diplomats usually lived'! Condesa was known for its art deco architecture and restaurants and cafes, and in recent years had become gentrified.

My curiosity was piqued immediately. It turned out to be a house in Calle Tacámbaro which had been designed by the well-known Mexican architect Enrique Norten. We were told that Norten had been living there (it was his family home) and that he was moving to the United States. The three-storey house was built in the Mexican modernist style, with a concrete facade, minimalist design, polished wooden floors, loads of storage and lots of light. It was built on a small block, had a terrace and a small garden, and was very clever in its use of space. For me, it was in a great neighbourhood, it seemed ideal for a family, had good security features (an important consideration for me, given that I would be alone in Mexico City with the children for much of the time) and, importantly, was within the embassy's rent ceiling and had no maintenance issues! I liked it immediately and without hesitation said we would like to rent it. We moved in shortly afterwards and, as the house had many built-in features, including beds, cupboards and shelving, we were able to put much of the embassy-issued heavy, dark-brown Parker style furniture – which did not in any way go with the minimalist style of the house – into storage.

We were less lucky with our car. Word had gotten around that a new family was coming to post and we were beseeched with people wanting to sell us cars, both new and second hand. I could not afford a new car and then we made a big mistake – we bought the first second-hand car that was offered to us. It was a khaki green 1993 Chrysler Spirit. It was a big American car, sold to us by the mechanics who serviced the embassy vehicles, who were affectionately known as the Dodgy Brothers. Because they were the mechanics used by the embassy, we assumed we could trust them. They told us that it was a very good car and that we could get it for a very good price. Not knowing anything about the second-hand car market in Mexico City and being in too much of a hurry, we immediately agreed to the asking price. No sooner had we agreed to pay the asking price, we realised that we had paid too much and that there were newer vehicles, at better prices, to be had. But, we were committed. The car was delivered and it was fine – at first.

Within a few weeks, however, we realised it was a gas-guzzling car which was difficult to manoeuvre and park. And then we had the first of many breakdowns when one day – driving along Avenida Revolución, a major arterial road in the south of Mexico City – smoke started billowing from the bonnet and, in the middle of heavy traffic, the car ground to a halt. We had to abandon our plans for the day, while our car was towed to the workshop. This happened on many occasions and I became well-known to the local taxi company in Condesa on the days when my car was in the Dodgy Brothers' workshop *en servicio* and I had to take taxis to and from work.

Probably our most memorable breakdown occurred one Saturday afternoon when – after returning from a day on the boats on the canals of Xochimilco with some friends who were visiting from Australia – we were driving along the Periférico, a major ring road in Mexico City, in heavy traffic. Smoke started to billow from the bonnet of the car and, as the car struggled up a hill, it gradually came to a halt – in the middle of the road. Drivers around us became annoyed and blasted their horns, but eventually a couple of kind people assisted us in pushing the car off the road. We pondered what to do. We did not have a mobile phone and there was no public telephone in sight. Then, almost miraculously, a man with a bag of tools appeared out of nowhere. Speaking to me in Spanish, he said that he could fix our vehicle, but that he didn't have the parts he needed. If we gave him some money, he said he would be able to buy them and – to prove that we could trust him – said that he would leave his own tools as a surety or guarantee that he would come back. Conrad opened his wallet and handed over several hundred pesos. He said he would be back in about 20 minutes.

My guests from Australia and I decided to go for a coffee and Conrad waited with the car. He waited and he waited. A few people came by to offer help, but Conrad said it was fine and that someone was helping us. By the time we came back from our coffee, there was still no sign of the man. A couple of passers-by suggested that maybe the man was not coming back, but we insisted that we were fine – someone was helping us. We waited and we waited...

After two or three hours, there was still no sign of the man and then, out of nowhere, another man with a bag of tools appeared and offered to help. We realised that we had been scammed by the first man and told the man that we didn't need any help. By this time, the car had cooled down and Conrad tried to start the engine – reluctantly, it kicked-off. We bundled back into the car and started to drive back to Condesa on the Periférico. In order to keep the engine cool, Conrad turned it off as we went down inclines and then turned it back on when we went uphill. This worked for a while until the car started to shudder and we were stopped by a policeman who blew his whistle and waved his arms, frantically beckoning us to get off the road. We tried to explain what had happened and so the policeman accompanied us, on foot, to a nearby garage. The garage organised a tow-truck and we were towed – five of us sitting in the car at the back of the tow-truck at a 45 degree angle – all the way back to Condesa. Apart from occasional stares from other people on the road at the sight of five people sitting at an angle of 45 degrees in a car being towed, we arrived home without further incident, some hours later than originally planned.

In the embassy, my responsibilities included seeking to resolve barriers to market access for Australian goods and services, securing access to the Mexican market for Australian live cattle, finalising a double taxation agreement between Australia and Mexico, public diplomacy and cultural relations. When the Ambassador was away, I acted as Head of Mission and attended various official events and receptions on his behalf.

We worked closely with the Mexican Department of Agriculture and met from time to time to discuss live cattle. Mexico imported livestock from Australia, but they could only come from the southern part of Australia because of the prevalence of Bluetongue disease in the north. Cattle from northern Australia could be exported to Mexico, but they had to be kept in the southern part of Australia prior to export, if they were to meet Mexico's stringent requirements.

On my first day of work at the embassy, I had to go to a meeting at the Mexican Department of Agriculture with a group of Australian vets to discuss Mexico's import requirements. As was to happen occasionally, I was asked to interpret, as the Australian vets did not speak Spanish, the Mexican officials spoke little or no English, and the embassy did not have an interpreter. Within minutes, I became fluent in Spanish veterinary terminology and phrases such as *lengua azul* (Spanish for Bluetongue disease). Every now and again, however, a puzzled or slightly annoyed look from one of the vets would tell me that my veterinary interpretation skills were perhaps lacking in some respects and, in other circumstances, could have potentially derailed the negotiations for a protocol for the importation of Australian cattle into Mexico.

Mexico also exported a lot of cattle and grains to the United States. One day our contacts in the Mexican Department of Agriculture invited a colleague from the New Zealand embassy and I to visit the US-Mexico border area to see first-hand some Mexican agricultural export facilities. We took a very early morning flight from Mexico City to Monterrey and then changed planes for a flight to Nuevo Laredo in the Mexican state of Tamaulipas, where we landed at the Quetzalcóatl International Airport and were met by our Mexican hosts.

I had only ever heard of Laredo – the town on the Texas side – through the 1950s North American cowboy show *Laredo*, with it grainy images of grey cowboys in black and white hats, and so I was curious to see what the real Laredo was like. As soon as we arrived, we were whisked-off in a four-wheel drive and headed for the US-Mexican border.

'We're going to cross the border. We hope you brought your passports?', asked one of our Mexican hosts.

We had not known this was the plan, but fortunately we had our passports. We nodded and proudly patted out bags – passports, check! Our vehicle soon joined the longest queue of trucks I had ever seen, all waiting to be checked and approved for entry into the United States. We were stationary most of the time, although every now and again our vehicle would lurch forward a few metres and, from time to time, because our car had Mexican government plates, we were able to jump parts of the queue. I had never seen so many trucks lined-up and I wondered if any carried undocumented people hidden away and whether the US border control would open-up and inspect every truck to see what cargo it carried.

We were surely in a for a long wait, but there was nothing to do other than to try to be patient, something I have always found hard at the best of times. With the early start from Mexico City – coupled with the heat and carbon monoxide fumes from so many vehicles revving noisily and impatiently on the spot – I slipped in and out of consciousness, occasionally disturbed by the intermittent cacophony of car and truck horns. As soon as someone honked their horn, everyone else would follow suit and somehow the horns on Mexican cars seemed to make the loudest, ugliest, most discordant sounds I had ever heard.

We waited...and we waited...and we waited...and I wondered why on Earth anyone would ever want to go to the United States. After a very long time, we reached the border and were waved through – no checks for us, no questions asked.

After passing a humongous sign which said 'WELCOME TO THE UNITED STATES OF AMERICA' and seeing that there was no traffic going in the opposite direction to Mexico, from the other side of the border, we knew we were in the United States – Laredo, Texas.

By now it was lunch-time and our hosts asked us where we wanted to eat. We had no idea where to eat in Laredo and so our hosts decided we should try a Mexican restaurant. It was a large barn of a place, with a selection of the heaviest, most fatty Mexican and Tex-Mex food I had ever seen, served fast-food food style in enormous portions from various serving stations; a kind of Mexican truckers' road-house. Big men wearing big hats and boots strode around with plates heaped high with food – truckers' fare. Not a soul spoke English and my New Zealand colleague and I stood out. We were the *güeras*, the Mexican term for white or foreign women. I struggled through what was a very unmemorable meal and then it was time for our official program to begin.

'We are going to take you to an abattoir first... so you can see how Mexican slaughter houses comply with international standards.'

My colleague, who was vegetarian, gasped. I drew breath. We had not signed-up for this.

'Is that okay?'

We both nodded – clearly, we should have asked for the proposed visit program before we came. We had no option, but to go along.

I made a note to myself: 'never accept any invitation unless you know exactly what you are accepting'. And then a second: 'always make sure you know what's in the program in advance'.

Back in the four wheel-drive we were whisked away at great speed to a meat handling facility in what appeared to be the middle of the desert. We were welcomed by the manager and were then taken to the first stop – a giant freezer. As we reached the entry, polar jackets, hats and gloves were thrust into our hands.

'You will need these,' we were told sternly by one of the staff, as we stepped into the facility and felt the temperature plummet by about 50 degrees within a matter of minutes. Images of B-grade horror movies conjured in my mind; what would happen if we accidentally got trapped in here? A chill ran-up my spine – I banished the thought.

After a quick tour of several rooms of the freezer, where we were shown boxes of hermetically sealed meat which we were told had been 'produced in Mexico, but manufactured to the highest US standards', it was time to go.

That wasn't so bad, I heaved a sigh of relief.

But the worst was still to come.

'We're going back to the Mexican side now and we're going to show you a meat processing facility. We hope you don't mind, but you're going to join a party of meat inspectors.'

My colleague gasped. 'This is the abattoir he mentioned before. We are going to cow Auschwitz!'

The next day started out better. We were told we were going to a grain-handling facility on the US-Mexican border. We had breakfast, packed-up and checked-out of the hotel. We were taken to the facility, just outside of the town, which was on a railway line and as close to the border as it could possibly be. The railway line stretched across the Rio Grande to the other side – the United States.

'Would you like to walk out to the border?' our Mexican hosts asked.

We thought we were on the border.

'No, you can walk right out to the border line. It's just out there, on the railway line. You can walk right up to the line. It's perfectly safe,' we were told.

We stepped gently onto the railway line and walked out to the border. We had to be very careful, because there were large gaps between the seemingly ancient railway sleepers, which creaked as we stepped from one to another. We reached the middle and there was the border, a line painted in white. On one side was painted the word MEXICO and, on the other, UNITED STATES OF AMERICA.

'Now be careful,' someone called from behind.

I turned around and, as I did, my shoe fell from my foot. As if in slow motion, it circled down several hundred metres to the river below.

I gasped. I did not have a spare pair of shoes and we had to catch a plane back to Mexico City in a couple of hours.

'I've lost my shoe!' I shouted.

One of the Mexican agriculture officials said they would go down to the river to look for it. On the other side of the river, we could see men with binoculars and pistols looking at us intently – the US border patrol. The idea of sending someone to look for my shoe, which by now no doubt would have been washed down the river, struck me as being dangerous and pointless; I felt awkward and embarrassed.

'No need,' I said. 'Can we please just find a shop and maybe I can buy a new pair of shoes?'

After visiting several shops in a desperate search to find shoes that would fit my feet, which were larger than those of the average Mexican woman, we found some that would get me back to Mexico City and were on our way. After this episode, I always wore 'sensible shoes' and had a spare pair, just in case.

One of the hardest things about being on posting was being alone with the children for much of the time. The working week was fine; I would go to work every day, take Jesse – and also later Amelia – to the Peterson School in Lomas de Chapultepec, where they attended a pre-school Montessori program, and then drive to work. Because we could never get ourselves organised to get out of the house early, we always seemed to hit peak for traffic (or maybe it was always peak hour in Mexico) and be bumper-to-bumper. Every day we passed some government buildings with an enormous Mexican flag and I was somewhat surprised one day to hear Jesse shout from the back seat, *¡viva México!* From that day on, every time we passed or saw a Mexican flag, Jesse's hand would shoot up in the air and he would shout *¡viva México!*

As I was at work a lot of the time, the children learnt Spanish from Rosa and another woman by the name of Lupis, who had been recruited by Rosa to help with the children and the house. Neither spoke any English and so the children learnt Spanish quickly. They would babble away in Spanish in the back-seat, as we inched through the morning traffic. Rosa cooked Mexican food for all of us (she always asked what she should cook for the children and I always responded that she should prepare whatever she liked) and the children – especially Jesse – developed a taste and love for rice, *frijoles y tortillas*.

I would be quite busy during the day with my job, dealing with tasks that had come in from the department in Canberra, accompanying the Ambassador on calls and then writing-up the reports of the meetings, and on occasion having lunch with colleagues. I would then come home in the evenings, relieve Rosa and Lupis of the task of caring for the children, and then have some time with Jesse and Amelia. By the time I got home, it would already be quite late and the children were often tired from their own days. I would play with them for a bit and then settle them for bed.

Rosa would return to her village on Saturdays and come back on Monday mornings, often with an enormous bag of washing. The washing machine seemed to run constantly throughout the week and we went through copious amounts of laundry detergent and fabric softener. I think she was probably running her own laundry business on the side. I didn't mind, as I was very reliant on her turning-up every Monday morning before I went to work and always felt happy when I heard the key turn in the door as she let herself in.

On the weekends, I would try to think of things I could do with the children, which often included visiting friends with children of similar ages or going shopping or to the children's museum. One of my biggest fears was losing the children in Mexico City! I was not worried about kidnapping, just that one of the children would run off and we would lose him or her in the crowd. One day Jesse ran off in a supermarket. Amelia was in a stroller, which I frantically wheeled up and down the aisles in search of Jesse. A few minutes later a Mexican couple appeared, holding a flailing child and asked if he was mine. I was relieved, but realised how easy it would be for a small child to slip away and disappear into the largest city in the world. I soon learnt that other mothers also held this fear! Before long, life had settled into a rhythm, which ebbed and flowed with the visits of Conrad, my parents, other family members and friends, and travel within Mexico, sometimes for work and occasionally for pleasure.

My posting was cut short by a promotion and I found myself in Canberra again. It was with a mix of emotions that I prepared to leave. On the one hand, it had been hard with Conrad commuting and being alone with the children much of the time. On the other, I had enjoyed the posting and had made some great friends. But such is life – things begin, things end and one moves on. It would be many years before I would return to Mexico again.

Tijuana freeway

Jacqueline Buswell

A figure moves in the corner of my eye
unclear   unfocussed   yet I know him
the swing of the hips, the ranchero hat
a Mexican campesino   heading north

cars speed past him as he walks
against all regulations
along the freeway   towards THE LINE:
an ugly tin fence and a parallel
higher barrier

Border Patrol vans are parked across
the arid hillocks of the no-man's-land
beyond THE LINE

sky darkens   the figure fades
first the hips   then the hat
he begins his turn to play
run and hide   crouch and wait

in a wood-slat hut with a leaking roof
Grandma works at the mud-brick stove
shapes the dough and cooks tortillas
hushes a child   kindles the flame

the waiting mother
tends a field of corn and squash
after a while she straightens
hands resting on her lower back

she gazes north
mutters something to herself
adjusts her own ranchero hat
bends again to work
plants marigolds for November

Mexico remembered

Lilit Thwaites

LILIT ŽEKULIN THWAITES is an award-winning Melbourne-based literary translator and an honorary research fellow in contemporary Spanish literature at La Trobe University. She won the 2015 inaugural Multicultural NSW Early Career Translator Prize, has received several travel grants and residencies associated with her translation work and, in 2016, was awarded the Spanish Order of Civil Merit for her promotion of Spanish culture in Australia. Her book-length translations include the bestselling *The Librarian of Auschwitz* (Antonio Iturbe, 2017 and 2019), *Australian Connection* (multiple authors, 2019), and two futuristic novels by Rosa Montero, *Tears in Rain* (Rosa Montero, 2012), and its sequel, *Weight of the Heart* (2016). Translations of short stories, essays and the occasional poem have been published in various journals and anthologies. She regularly presents sessions at writers' festivals, gives lectures on Spanish-related and translation topics, organises visits to Australia by Spanish-speaking writers, and features as a commentator on matters Spanish in the media. Her profile can be found at: https://scholars.latrobe.edu.au/display/lmthwaites.

MEXICO 1

My first ever encounter with Mexico is México DF in the early 1970s. A good friend and fellow-PhD student in Toronto has organised for me to spend four or five days with a friend of his in DF, and off I go. I have to say that my clearest memories have less to do with the sights, sounds and smells of Mexico and considerably more to do with trying to locate a missing suitcase. On that score, thank goodness, I have a local to help me navigate airport and airline '*burocracia*' – 'wait a day or two' from the Mexican airline company, followed by 'not our fault, since you travelled on a Canadian flight'; 'not our fault' from the Canadian company, 'we were only acting for the Mexican airline'. So, no suitcase, and no offer of the supposedly obligatory $50 to buy emergency supplies until the day before I am due to fly back home!

But my Mexican friend more than makes up for the behaviour of his bureaucratic *compatriotas*. In between endless lengthy negotiations, he not only takes me to all the main tourist spots, but to many locally enjoyed highlights too, including colourful craft markets, back alleys, and street eateries, but also provides me with the opportunity to experience daily life with a welcoming middle-class Mexican family...

I am stunned and overwhelmed by the sights and sounds of a city and of a country about which I have so far only read books and seen films. None of this can prepare me for the totally entwined *tres culturas*, Chapultepec park, Teotihuacán, the Basílica of the Virgen de Guadalupe, the hanging gardens, the shy smiles and kindness of the people; nor for the poverty, the dirt, the noise, the pollution, the clear distinctions between social and racial classes and yet, *la gachupina* (yes, the Spanish accent of the imperialist colonisers) is hooked! In the end, it doesn't matter that I get home days before my suitcase is found – at an airport on the east coast of Canada! I know I will be back.

MEXICO 2

My second visit (1999) is somewhat longer and begins in Querétaro with a conference about Spanish and Latin American Women Writers. The conference centre is 'out of this world': a magnificently restored former-hacienda-now-hotel with beautiful gardens, a swimming pool (never did find out who stole my brand-new swimsuit from the balcony railing!), and even a restored *capilla* whose only function now is to be decorative. There is a little time to explore the sights, sounds and tastes of old Querétaro, with its colonial and baroque architecture, until the closing event, which is held in the magnificently restored theatre. Again, I am struck by the quirky sculptures, the art galleries with strikingly unusual offerings, and the racial and class distinctions – this time in a more upmarket environment – but in addition, by that same demonstration of pride in indigenous heritage and pre-colonial cultures.

And then a few short days back in México DF, staying with an Australian diplomat and her family – the chance to see and experience the city from a slightly different perspective, through the eyes of an informed foreigner. This time I have arrived armed with lots of advice from colleagues who know Mexico well – 'only take these cabs, never take those cabs'; 'don't use ATMs in these areas'; 'don't get on or off at these metro stations (no matter how impressive the stations filled with excavated treasures might be), but make sure you do visit XX *barrios* and XX *plazas*...' I still remember walking down ancient streets where I had to go down six or seven stone steps to reach what used to be street level, before entering a church leaning drunkenly to one side. And the amazing *Casa de los Azulejos* where I have a cup of coffee while admiring the architecture and tilework. And I'll never forget those horrendously realistic statues of Christ and various martyrs displayed alongside beautiful, but at times barely visible, works of art. Two definite highlights: the Diego Rivera frescoes, and the interior of the Palacio de Bellas Artes, a highlight to be trumped next time round, it turns out. A different – or perhaps simply a changing – Mexico altogether, but then so am I.

MEXICO 3

Mexico the third time round (2005) is full of surprises, for three reasons: I'm not travelling on my own; we're staying with a friend and expert on all things Mexican in his rented apartment in Coyoacán;

and I have just come from another conference on Women Writers in Tegucigalpa, Honduras (an even more impoverished and troubled country than Mexico), followed by an almost tourist-free trip to the Mayan ruins in Copán. The contrast could not be greater between the Mayan ruins where art, sculpture, and artistic creativity were clearly centre-stage, and Teotihuacán (again, three days after Copán) where I once again feel that the focus was clearly on demonstrating power and domination via architecture on a grand (almost fascist) scale, with the artistic definitely seen as having a minor role.

But a moment's reflection here on Coyoacán and Frida Kahlo, and that extraordinary house/museum she shared with Diego. I had recently explored aspects of Frida's life and her art for an illustrated paper on an exiled Catalan-Chilean artist, Roser Bru. Bru had discovered Kahlo's art in a US magazine in the dress shop where she was working when she first arrived in Chile. She was so taken by it that she explored many of Kahlo's themes and styles in her own drawings and sketches. But no amount of slides and photographs could prepare me for the real thing – wandering the streets that Frida trod, and seeing Frida's art in her own house. Another surprise: México DF feels much cleaner and safer (not that I'd ever felt particularly threatened on earlier visits, I hasten to add) as we travel the crowded buses and subway again and visit places I have been to before. In Chapultepec Park we are fortunate to see the flying acrobats spinning atop what looks like a very tall maypole, and to explore the incredible museum of anthropology. And then, unexpectedly, another visit to the Palacio de Bellas Artes, this time to see a performance of the *Ballet Folklórico de México*, preceded by the incredible play of lights on the Tiffany glass stage curtain – Mexico's two volcanoes on display, as if from dawn to dusk. Again, I am dazzled by the art on display in galleries and streets, the mix of architectural styles and cultures, the warmth of the people, and the food, colours and sounds of this city built on such ancient foundations, cultures and traditions – a city that seems never to stop nor to sleep.

MEXICO 4

A short 'official business' trip (2006) connected with my university's overseas exchange programmes, accompanied by several colleagues. Another old but 'new' city for me – Guadalajara – and another chance to see parts of Mexico from the air and by road. Other colleagues have the more important roles on this trip; I mainly provide the Spanish and some information and questions about the languages and international relations on offer. There's time to observe and enjoy the benefits that come with such trips, including delicious food, a chance to visit parts of buildings and galleries not open to ordinary tourists (amazing Orozco murals), and a glimpse, again, of how the locals see themselves and view 'others'. Apart from some common threads (that quirky street sculpture; friendly inhabitants), Guadalajara also presents yet another side of Mexico: different architecture and use of space, a different landscape, different natural light (much less pollution) and smells. And then it's back to México DF for a couple of days before the return flight, but it's a DF caught up in the highs and eventual lows of the final stages of a soccer World Cup. Everywhere we go, TVs and radios are blaring non-stop soccer, and Mexicans are either cheering and yelling (abusing referees, with an entirely different but equally recognisable vocabulary), or drowning their pain and sorrow – while still abusing the referees!

There is time only for a quick visit to new wonders (Museo de Arte Popular) and a few old favourites – the murals a little grimier, the old buildings a little more sunken, the parks, museums, bookshops, galleries and little craft shops still a joy... Time only to gain the impression that life is no easier for many of Mexico's inhabitants now than it was the first time I visited, a situation that looks unlikely to change in the near future.

MEXICO 5

Not an actual visit to Mexico, but an invitation to give a talk on an aspect of Mexico at a weekend series of talks and events organised in Armadale in 2007 by the CWA (Country Women's Association). Not being an expert on Mexico, I am somewhat surprised by the invitation, but it coincides with my reading Ana Lanyon's book about La Malinche, *Malinche's Conquest,* and some other books I have recently been reading that also mention this critical, and for some, treacherous figure in Mexico's history. It is a chance to revisit (my take on) aspects of Mexico's pre-colonial, colonial and post-colonial history as seen and portrayed through film, art (Frida Kahlo again) and literature (with a bit of history thrown in); and it proves a thoroughly enjoyable and informative experience, certainly for me and hopefully for my audience.

Mexico 6 down the track? – *ojalá!* There's still so much to explore and learn, from so many angles, and so many new and ongoing issues to discuss and experience. *¡¡Qué sea pronto!!*

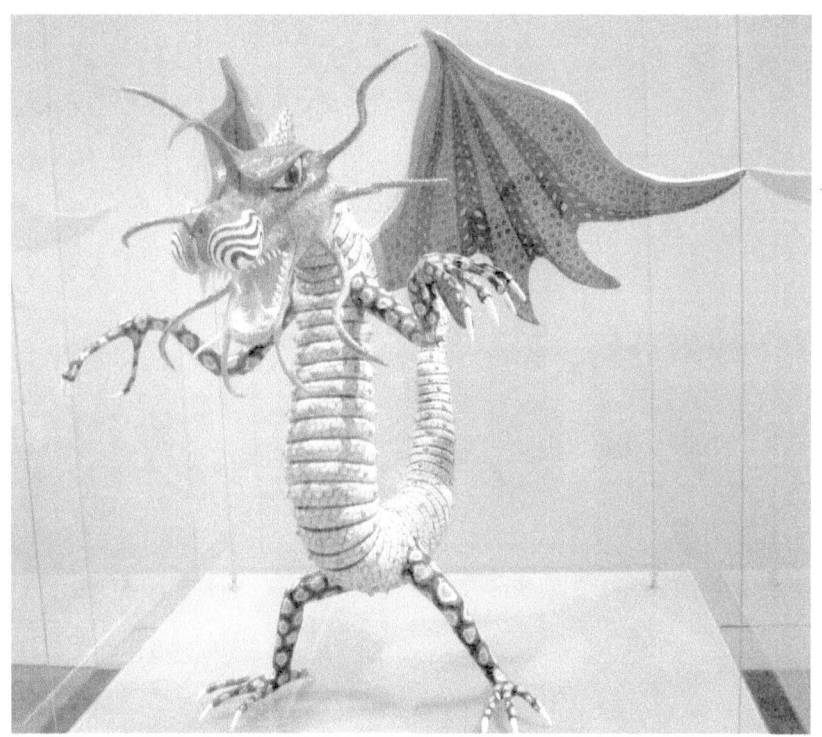

Photo: A wonderfully ferocious and colourful Mexican *alebrije* (imaginary animal).

My journey to *Misión México* and beyond

Pamela Jean Skuse

PAMELA SKUSE is the founder and director of the refuge *Misión México, Dando Amor, Vida y Esperanza A.C* and the surf project, *Misión Surf*, in southern Mexico. Pam came to Mexico in 2000 and has spent the last 20 years as the Mamá of the children's home. She has worked alongside her husband Alan and both have strived to make a difference in the lives of the children placed in their care. Pam's heart for disadvantaged children is huge and over the years she's found it extremely difficult to turn away children in need, to the point that at one stage the refuge was bursting at the seams. As a more structured refuge was created with a cap of 30 children, a more orderly life was generated with Pam delegating responsibilities, giving her time to plan additional programs to enhance the children's lives. Although the refuge took on a new form, it never lost its family orientation. Pam is also the mother of nine children, grandmother to 17 grandchildren and great grandmother to one, all living in Australia. You can visit the *Misión* websites at: www.lovelifehope.com or www.misionsurfmexico.com.

In November 2000 my husband Alan and I, along with our 15-year-old daughter Hannah, came to Mexico to help establish a refuge for children in the border city of Tapachula, Chiapas. Tapachula is situated approximately 18 kilometres from the Guatemalan border and has a population of around 350,000. Being a border city it has numerous problems, such as drug trafficking, crime, violence, illegal immigration and poverty. Our daughter Brooke, who was 19 years old, had been living in the southern city on the west coast the year prior, and helped out at a children's refuge. On her return to Australia she shared with us the great need in the perilous city. A seed was sown in our hearts and before long we were on a plane headed for a new volunteering adventure for a twelve-month period.

Within the first six months the organisation that we came to assist with the establishment of the refuge shut its doors virtually overnight and we were left with the huge decision as to whether to stay in Mexico and continue the work that we were doing, or head back home to Australia.

Although we didn't have many children at that stage we had grown attached to the ones in our care and the thought of them going back to the welfare department, and the possible outcome of them ending up on the streets, convinced us that we needed to stay. Without any financial support, other than our own personal savings, we resumed our work and began writing letters to family and friends to seek their support.

Now, 20 years later, we are still living and working with Mexico's disadvantaged children. It's been 20 years of service and sacrifice; 20 years of loving the unloved. We have built more than a home for children; we have created a family. Although it's been an incredibly difficult journey, we have tried to fill the home with an abundance of love, a quality life, and hope for the future.

It certainly hasn't been easy and we have had our fair share of heartache. Living and working with damaged children can take its toll on you, there's no doubt about that. One rebellious teen in a family is hard enough, but at one stage we had 28 teenagers living under the same roof; 28 teenagers pushing boundaries and breaking rules. It was during that period of time that I wrote a poem and in one verse I wrote, 'If I knew how much my heart would ache, would I have ventured here for their sake? The demands of life, the need to escape, oh my God, I beg you, not to forsake.' It was a cry for help during an incredibly difficult time. But life goes on, and I had to pick myself up and pull myself together, and remind myself of why we were here.

We were not in Mexico as tourists; we were in this country to make a difference in the lives of the forgotten ones. We had been called to this land to encourage and inspire the children that were placed in our care to set goals and reach for the stars.

Over the years we have helped hundreds of children, making a difference in big ways, and in small ways, but making a difference all the same. There have been many highs and many lows, and in reality, not all of our stories have had happy endings.

Every year living in Mexico has brought with it a vast amount of trials and tribulations in the work that we do and 2020 has been no exception. In March of 2020 we were devastated with the illness and death of one of our teens. The seriousness of Vidalicia's illness transpired quickly and after just three weeks in hospital our sweet Vida was gone. The grief that I have felt has been overwhelming and I am still coming to terms with it. The Covid-19 pandemic that followed has caused fear and anxiety. Being in isolation has given me a sense of security, and I am certainly happy that the children have been kept safe, but it has also created a sense of sadness being separated from loved ones back home, not knowing if I will ever see my family again.

Tapachula is constantly hot, and incredibly humid. It is definitely not a tourist destination. We have struggled over the years with the language, the heat, separation from family and the stresses of making ends meet, and that's just a few of the hardships that we have borne. Though, in saying that, I am thankful that over the past 20 years we've endured, through the good times and the bad; through sickness and health, and unbelievable grief. Yet, all of these discomforts and difficulties have built me to be the person that I am today and I am so grateful that I have had the opportunity to be a part of the journey of so many.

Now we are witnessing triumphs that cause my heart to soar. Children who were orphaned, abandoned, starved, neglected, beaten and sexually abused have overcome the unimaginable and have graduated from school and universities with a wide range of degrees. I am proud to say that we at *Misión México* have witnessed many of our young adults who have graduated to become business administrators, a doctor, a lawyer, biotechnologists, computer techs, social workers, a

Photo: Encouraging *Misión México* girls to surf has been a huge focus for the surf program.

Photo: Children from the refuge gain confidence on bodyboards before progressing to surfboards. Surfing began in 2003 as an activity for *Misión México, Dando Amor, Vida y Esperanza A.C.* with a couple of 'nipper' rescue boards that had been donated by the Australian Sunshine Beach Surf Life Saving Club.

language teacher and a police investigator. We also have great satisfaction as we witness the dreams of the subsequent generations develop and their strong character traits lean toward becoming chefs, teachers, marines and a politician. Another satisfaction is to observe some of our young adults commence families of their own in loving, stable environments, something that they had been denied prior to coming to live at the refuge. To witness this change in each individual, while remembering the lives of poverty and violence that they came from, fills me with humility and a grand admiration of each young person's resilience and determination to conquer the negative memories of their previous lives and strive to become the best that they can be.

I'm a dreamer and my dreams have kept me going over the years and have given me the will to fight on when it seemed too hard to continue. One dream that I had many years ago was to develop a surf culture in our local area. With Alan being a surfer from the age of 15 years, and with the refuge being built relatively close to the beach, we had the perfect opportunity to introduce the children to the 'stoke' of surfing. This sport activity, that was unheard of in the area when we started, would not only become a form of enjoyment for the whole *Misión México* family, it also became a therapy and has helped the children and young adults overcome the traumas that haunt them from the past. Not only did this activity help our children and youth emotionally, they were proud to be a part of *Misión México* and wouldn't hesitate to don a *Misión México* t-shirt to advertise where they came from.

Since the initial dream, the surf culture has grown to where we now have a surf school right on the beach of Puerto Madero. *Misión Surf* is open to the public, enabling *tapachultecos* and people from far and wide to visit and partake in the surf culture, which in turn, helps the project to become self-sustainable. Additionally, the surf project provides free swimming, surf, English, and the occasional art classes to the local impoverished community.

One of our young men, who was one of the rebellious teens mentioned earlier, has come back to *Misión Surf* after eight years away and is now in a management position within the surf project. His surf skills had gone a little rusty due to his absence, but over the past two years he has become as sharp as he was before he left.

Many years ago, I organised to send this young man, along with his older brother, to Puerto Escondido in Oaxaca for a short period of time to learn the skill of surfboard repairs. After he fled the love and security that the refuge provided him, and travelled down dangerous paths, I wondered if my enthusiasm in providing him with such skills was a failed effort on my part. Now, with this man finding stability once again, not only have those skills that he learned so long ago become a beneficial tool in his development, the investment is now bringing rewards to *Misión Surf*.

Alan and I are now at a point in time where we are ready to step back and place this incredible project in the capable hands of others. Alan, who is currently 70-years-old, is still surfing with the kids. He is a legend in their eyes and a fine example of what fatherhood is about. I am now almost 68 years old and ready to spend more time with our nine children (six biological, two adopted and one foster) plus 17 grandchildren, and one great grandchild in Australia. The children of *Misión México* will continue to be in our hearts, and both Alan and I will continue to visit the refuge as long as we are able and work for the betterment of the project.

Mexico will always be a special place to me. Over the years I have fallen in love with its ethnicity and traditions. I love the colours, the food and the richness that the Mexican culture offers. What I thought was strange in my initial years in Mexico has now become part of my being and I will be encouraging our eight Mexican/Australian grandchildren to learn about their heritage.

Great things have been accomplished over the years and I am proud and honoured to have been part of this incredible journey along with my husband and our incredible team.

Cathy Carey: A tribute

Jenny Cooper

Cathy grew up in Sydney's Sutherland shire during the sixties. After starting an arts degree at the University of New South Wales in the 1970s and juggling her study with campaigns against the Vietnam War, she developed an interest in Latin America and Spanish, and left Sydney to explore Mexico. She stayed for eight years.

Cathy learnt Spanish quickly and spoke fluently, almost without an accent, her language skills were exceptional. She could communicate and engage in debate with renowned Mexican journalists, as well as with my mother-in-law from the north of Mexico, the peasants in the mountains of Guerrero and townsfolk from Xico in Veracruz where she took up residence.

Cathy witnessed the poverty and richness of village life working as a teacher while also writing articles for the local newspapers in Jalapa and taking photographs. She travelled widely and explored the depths of Mexican culture and its people as evidenced in the photos she has left with us. The best photos I have of my family members and especially my children whom she cared for many a time were taken by Cathy.

A gallery of the National Auditorium housed an exhibition of Cathy's photos from February to April 1982, along with those of other Mexican and foreign resident photographers. One of her photos was selected as part of the prestigious and highly competitive *Bienal de Fotografía*, an event which still takes place in Mexico today and dates back to the first photographic exhibition in 1979.

Returning to Australia, Cathy completed a master's degree in anthropology while also raising her daughter Valentina and working as a Spanish interpreter at Lidcombe Workers Health Centre.

In the late 1980s, Cathy began what became a 20-year career with SBS TV, first as a Spanish subtitler and then as a journalist and researcher with programs including Dateline and Insight. A piece Cathy researched on native title and the Larrakia people won a UN media award, as did a Dateline story on torture in Spain.

Perhaps the most famous TV series which Cathy subtitled was *Cuna de Lobos* (Cradle of Wolves) a Mexican soap opera produced by Carlos Téllez for *Televisa* in 1986. The serial, about the struggle for power within a wealthy Mexican dynasty, was enormously popular in its native Mexico and was also a hit in several foreign countries, including Australia and Germany.

With artist Jane Naylor, she established the Leichhardt Academy of Style and Health – LASH for short – a group whose chief pursuits included random public art installations, political and social gatherings and occasional perambulations around Leichhardt during which complete strangers would be bailed up and congratulated on their dress sense or grammar.

Cathy made a last trip to Mexico to visit her beloved town of Xico after she had been diagnosed with cancer and was in remission. She was determined not to surrender to the disease and in her last years she worked in the Journalism and Media Research Centre at the University of New South Wales, which allowed her to keep researching and writing about an industry that at times fascinated and at times appalled her.

Cathy died of cancer in Sydney in 2011.

Photo: Cathy Carey – from the series *La boda 1981 (The wedding 1981)*, which received an honourable mention in the photographic competition, *Bienal de Fotografía*, held in 1982.

Photo: Cathy Carey.

Photo: Cathy Carey.

Photo: Cathy Carey.

Photo: Cathy Carey.

Just dancing

Jacqueline Buswell

Lo bailado nadie te lo quita
(Spanish proverb)
No-one takes away what you've danced

at first her life was wonder, play and dance
then slow years of maths, grammar
homework, sports days

another flash of dance and play
then the rushing years
love, life projects

debts chores holidays
and at any moment, randomly
loss and death

the thought of her own.
All the material, she saw, was fragile
could be gone in any brief disaster

only the dancing, they say
can't be taken
but later, panting up the stairs

she remembers the cumbia
give back, she demands
give me back the dancing!

Peg Job: A tribute

Jacqueline Buswell

Peg Job was an Australian woman who lived in Mexico in 1986-87 and who would surely have contributed to this anthology were she still alive. She was a talented writer and a woman keen to express her ideas, opinions and stories. Before she went to Mexico she wrote a book narrating the illness and death of her husband in *The Dying*, published by Redress Press in 1986.

Peg lived in Mexico for two years with her young son Jarrah to research her PhD project on Sexuality in Contemporary Mexican Women's Narrative (1970-87). That was when I met her, she lived in the same area around Ciudad Universitaria-Copilco as I did, and indeed, so did Jenny Cooper and her husband Juan. Peg received her PhD from the University of New South Wales and I went to that university's library to read her thesis.

She read the literature critically to discover how the women writers portrayed sexuality and discovered that the family was important in the construction of adult sexual attitudes, with the assumption that sexuality was heterosexual and reproductive. Some writers had begun to explore sexuality as a tool in the journey towards the self in their writing and Peg especially studied the work of Aline Pettersson in this regard. Other authors included Elena Urrutia, Elena Poniatowska, Rosario Castellanos, Ethel Krauze and Maria Luisa Puga.

Peg wrote in her thesis that her overwhelming impression from analysing the writings of dozens of Mexican women was that sexuality was not about pleasure but about possession – women being possessed by men, women possessing men and women wishing to be possessed. She wrote, 'this seems to be an extremely complex area of human desire, not entirely explicable within the theoretical frameworks so far devised around human sexuality'.

Other elements of sexuality perceived in the writings were the desire to merge with another and sexuality as a mechanism to escape solitude and alone-ness.

> It is rarely represented anywhere as a light-hearted recreational pursuit; even the 'one-night stand' is expected to produce 'more'. Women's sexuality is consistently represented as meaningful, even if the meanings vary.

When she returned from Mexico, Peg lived in Sydney and Canberra before settling in Braidwood, New South Wales. She had many jobs and occupations, friends and family. As editor of the journal of the Academy of Social Sciences in Australia, she co-ordinated many interesting issues, including a couple about Central Australia. She made at least two road trips to Alice Springs where she met specialists from many fields and invited them to write for the journal. I know this because Peg always wrote travelogues from her journeys, describing both highlights and down moments in the traveller's days. In 2013 she made a solo road trip around Australia.

I always missed these long group emails when she got home and wished she would report on her daily life from the home front too. The emails resumed when she embarked on her final courageous journey towards death, and she wrote to us about medical diagnosis and treatment, the support from family and friends, while she could.

Peg died of cancer in Braidwood in February 2017, aged 71. On her tombstone it says:

PEG LOVED WORDS AND OTHER LIVING THINGS.

Livin' la vida loca

Lulu Honeywild

LULU HONEYWILD was born in Brisbane and completed a Bachelor of Arts and concurrent Diploma of Languages at the University of Melbourne. She has lived for most of her 20s in Guadalajara and is currently working on various projects, including a natural skincare line, multiple local design stores, a clothing line as well as continuing her modelling career. She sees herself staying in Mexico.

True to the song title *Livin' la vida loca*, life here in Mexico can be a little crazy.

I'm 25, living in Guadalajara, Jalisco. The second largest city in Mexico, home state to mariachi music and tequila, and the place that has become my home over the last few years.

I'm becoming an adult here. I arrived for the first time in 2013, 20 years old and so very green. I knew nothing – about Mexico or myself, and was armed with little more than basic Spanish and a stomach full of nerves and bravado.

I expected to complete my six months on exchange, travel a little, return to Australia and continue my life there. Maybe get an internship back at home in a charity, continue my studies, complete a master's degree... follow the road mapped out for me.

I never expected to be living in one of the most beautiful streets in Guadalajara, Calle Libertad – lined with trees with eyes painted on them. Walking my dog in the morning and night, building a life here.

I never expected to have a successful career modelling, to get recognised in the local OXXO (Mexican version of 7/11), to have my face on billboards all over the country or to be flown to other cities to be a part of national campaigns for Mexican designers and brands.

I never expected to have a small business, a design store that I fill with local independent brands. Never expected to have faced the challenges of building it up piece by piece until it became something to be truly proud of, a business that supports local, ethical design.

But I guess that's what becoming an adult is as well. Accepting that your plans may change completely, your life may change completely, that you never know what is ahead of you and all you can do is throw yourself into life and go with what flows for you.

My first year here was puppy love, parties and travel (and I suppose a little studying as well). A beautiful, innocent time where I absorbed experiences like a hungry sponge.

It was magic.

I spent the first few months in a happy haze. I had rented a small room in a student house in the centre of town, an hour away from my university but centred in the busy, fun, more 'authentic' part of town.

Exchange students arrive in Mexico from wealthier countries, such as France, Germany, Sweden, etc. They're cashed up and they see this country as a place where anything goes, which can probably be attributed to the depiction of Mexico in much of America's pop culture as a lawless paradise.

In comparison to what I've been told about past years, there are now a great number of exchange programs with many countries. In my first semester in 2013, we were over 300 from more than 15 countries in my university alone. I imagine that number is even higher now six years later.

We gorged ourselves on *tacos, tortas ahogadas* (literally translated as drowned sandwiches), *micheladas, aguachile, ceviche* and *tequila*. We discovered a Mexico that had not been presented to us via media stories of drugs and violence and gangs. The rich culture of Mexican cuisine is nothing akin to the Old El Paso hard taco kit that my Mum picked up at Woollies.

I was surprised by how exchange students were now a business opportunity for young Mexicans, people around my age had created businesses to cater to what we wanted, they organised parties with cover charges, had share houses which gave them income by providing easy living arrangements to international students and organised trips to harder to reach places that young students might not have been exposed to.

This now surprises me less, as I now see this entrepreneurial spirit in many of my age bracket here. Mexico is a country of much opportunity, it is in the process of a hyper-speed version of globalisation and many small businesses influenced by foreign ideas are thriving. Café culture is booming, local design is becoming popular and little boutique bars and restaurants are becoming more common.

Post-university I returned to Australia for a short time. I finished my degree, worked in a social research call centre for a time and filled my summer with festivals and plans with friends. Like many of us leaving university at such a young age, I had no idea what I really wanted to do and found myself disinterested in following the plan I had set out for myself.

I returned to Mexico to travel to places that I hadn't experienced like Puebla and the Yucatán peninsula. I also went up to Toronto, Boston and New York. And down to Colombia, Guatemala, Belize and finally Cuba.

Strangely enough in Cuba, a divine intervention of sorts led me back to Guadalajara. The Pope arrived in Cuba the day I was meant to leave on a flight and they closed a perimeter off around the airport to cars (something that, without internet, I was blissfully unconscious of!). And so instead of arriving for my flight on time, I had to walk 2km with my 25kg backpack past rows of Cubans with flags waiting for the Pope! One of my thongs kept breaking and it was stinking hot. When I finally arrived at the airport after some very frustrating negotiating with the airport staff, they put me onto a plane to Mexico City and from there, exhausted, I took a last minute flight to Guadalajara, deciding to rest a while in a familiar place after so much travelling.

Photo: Lulu Honeywild considers that modelling in Mexico has given her freedom and agency over her life.

I spent the next year and a half somewhat lost from myself. I didn't know what I wanted and spent more time on distractions than really putting effort into finding out what it was. I travelled between Guadalajara, Mexico City, Boston and Australia, not sure even where I wanted to be.

Modelling changed that. It gave me a reason to take more care of myself and a reason to see myself in a different light. As someone strong, driven, professional and hard working. To see a future where I could excel in a profession that I enjoy and to start to dream again about where else it could take me and what else could interest me. The modelling industry gets a very bad rap, and in many cases it can be damaging to a person. But for me, it has allowed me a freedom and agency over my life that has allowed me to grow into the person that I am today, and I give thanks for that.

Having this career gave me a reason to put down roots somewhere, to stop running between city and country, and to allow myself to grow in very different ways. Guadalajara is that place for me, and sometimes it feels more home than Australia. They say I speak Spanish like a *tapatía* (a person born in Guadalajara) and its true! Sometimes I even forget words in English because the language here is so comfortable to me!

I fell in love with the city during afternoon walks in spring, when the whole city blooms with flowers from Jacaranda, Golden Rain and Royal Poinciana trees.

Modelling also reconnected me to my childhood passion for the world of fashion, which led to me opening my own design store and starting to teach myself about fashion design. The movement of consuming local is relatively new in Mexico especially in comparison to Australia, but it is in a boom, and many Mexicans are moving away from foreign produced goods to support the many talented young people who are embracing their heritage and creating exciting new products that reflect the contemporary Mexican identity.

My city is a beautiful place; it's growing, so it can also be noisy and dangerous, and filled with dust from construction sites. But it's also exciting and every time that I think I know Mexico, I always end up discovering something new that challenges me to view this country and this city in a different light. I don't know if I'll stay forever, but I do know that it would take me forever to be able to understand everything here, to be able to truly be Mexican.

But I don't need to be Mexican to love Mexico. In fact, sometimes I am asked constantly by people why I am here and not in Australia – an idolised place for them. I simply respond that I love my home, but that I love it here too. It's true – I know Australia will always be there for me, but for now, here is home.

What not to do

Jennifer Perkin

JENNIFER PERKIN is Venezuelan-English. She was born in the United States, raised in Melbourne and has spent most of her adulthood in Central America, Mexico and the United Kingdom. She is co-founder of *Convivio*, a creative space in the heart of Oaxaca city that aims to be a nucleus for collaboration and exploration. Before *Convivio*, Jen combined her passions for journalism, music, food and travel in her work as a culture and travel writer. She is director of the *Trueque Festival*, a project that aims to foster a cultural exchange between Mexico and Australia through a shared love of coffee.

When I think about the first year-and-a-half in Oaxaca I think about hot sweaty municipal offices, spread out all over the city and invariably populated by slow moving, eye-contact-avoiding workers who seem to always be on a lunch break. I think about the elaborate waiting rituals in these ugly, beige buildings. Sometimes you wait in lines, sometimes write your name in books, sometimes you take a number, or sit or stand in uncomfortable locations. Sometimes you wait for hours just for the office to close before you are seen and then you have to do it all again the next day. Sometimes the office is randomly closed because of a protest, or an obscure holiday, or just because.

Even when you do get seen, the news is seldom good. Turns out you needed just one more photocopy, or you're in the wrong place. You've filled out the wrong form, the system is down today, the person who can help you is on holiday, or the computer simply says no.

But it's not like I ever thought it would be easy.

'Aren't you scared? Isn't it corrupt? Isn't it dangerous? How do you know it will work?'

None of these were bad questions, directed at me by almost everyone I knew or met, but they just weren't the questions that mattered to me. I wanted to do it so I was going to do it. After all, plenty of Mexicans do it every day! I trusted that it would work. And if it didn't, then I would do something else.

I also knew one thing, and that one thing became my mantra: if it was easy, everyone would be doing it.

Oaxaca is undeniably a special place. People fall for it hard, they get misty eyed about it, they swoon for it. I don't know a single person (expect perhaps my father) who hasn't been utterly seduced by the city, and yet compared to other places there are relatively few entirely foreign-owned businesses. Most foreigners I met in the city were either working remotely for companies overseas, freelance artists or writers, working for an NGO or essentially living in early retirement.

So, I set out to do what exactly what everyone knows not to do, Business 101: don't start a business with family members or loved ones. I started a business in a foreign country with my brother, his girlfriend AND my boyfriend. Only one of us spoke Spanish, me.

There's no manual, no blog, not even an online forum about how you go about doing something like that. You figure it out as you go along, or sometimes you just don't figure it out at all. We started off in Guatemala and ended up in Mexico. We started off with the idea of taking over an existing hostel and instead built an independent hotel / coworking space / gallery / cinema / creative hub. We started off with four people and quickly ended up with two, and then later just one, me.

It wasn't easy, and that's why no one was doing it.

The paperwork, the millions of photocopies, the outright lies, the open corruption, the slippery non-answers. None of this is unique to Mexican bureaucracy, but it does have its own special flavour in Mexico. One of the first cultural phenomena that I picked up on is what I call the 'need-to-know basis'. In Oaxaca, unless you ask a very specific set of questions, you will not receive the answers you are looking for.

Them – You cannot complete this paperwork at this office, you have to go to the one across town.

Me – But I just went there as you told me to and it was closed. There is a sign saying I need to come here.

Them – Yes, that's right, the other office is closed until the end of the year.

Me – So, you can complete my paperwork for me?

Them – No.

Me – So, how can I complete this paperwork?

Them – You will need to come back here between the hours of 12pm and 2pm.

Me – But that is when your office is closed for lunch.

Them – Yes.

It's like a game. One player holds all the answers and the other player needs to ask just the right combination of questions to unlock them. One of the first times I became aware of the 'need-to-know basis' game was when I was hiring someone for outdoor work. We had an initial meeting so he could survey the work needed and give me quote.

Me – So this is the quote for the entire job, including everything.

Him – Yes.

Me – Great, let's start on Monday.

Monday:

Him – I need some money to go and purchase materials.

Me – But I already gave you 50 per cent of what we agreed up front!

Him – Yes but that didn't include MATERIALS!

It is a painfully obvious statement but I just have to say it: Mexican bureaucracy is what the word Kafkaesque was invented for. I am certain Kafka spent some time in Oaxacan municipal offices. Once I spent almost a year working towards an official piece of paper that said we were allowed to use the building as a workspace, which is considered a low-risk usage. When I finally received the piece of paper it instead authorised me to use the building as a *Child Care Centre* of all things, considered a high-risk usage and requiring many more steps.

Me – How did this happen?

Them – Whoops. You will need to start the process again.

I know someone who had a new building constructed on her street and when it was completed it was given the exact same house number as hers. When she spoke to the local government, to point out the obvious directional and mail delivery issues, she was told *she* would have to apply for a brand new street number.

I could go on. The thing is, none of this is a big deal if you are happy to go with the flow. Mostly, I expected the unexpected, took a book with me to all official appointments and managed to laugh things off (if it was easy, everyone would be doing it). I joked that one day I would write the world's most boring book about my adventures in Mexican bureaucracy. Don't even ask me about the time I had to shit in a cup to get one particular piece of paper. This was a different and new country so of course things would be different and new. The only reason any of it is a problem is if you expect things to be another way. I tried, oh how I tried, to go with the flow. But my stubbornly Eurocentric and linear-thinking brain kept getting in the way. I wanted to do things the right way, the legal way, dot the i's, cross the t's, add the tilde's to every last ñ. It turns out, it doesn't work that way.

Months of getting all the appropriate licenses, permissions and slips, paying all the fees, filling out all the forms, getting all the lovely pieces of paper for my business. Then it turned out my neighbours were very, very powerful people who didn't like us and what we were doing, and they managed to get us shut down anyhow, illegally, using their contacts in the government.

It was only after fighting to be reopened, trying to get even more licences and permissions, being threatened again, that I eventually and by accident found out who I needed to pay off to stay open. So simple: you just pay off a government official to stay open. All those piles of photocopies, those treks across the city, all those maddening hours spent with dead-behind-the-eyes civil servants, and all I really needed was to know who to pay.

There are many, many more interesting and wonderful things that happened to me in those first years in Oaxaca. But if you ask me about starting an independent business in Oaxaca, this is my truth.

But I did it. And if it was easy, everyone would be doing it.

True story

Jacqueline Buswell

here is a pair of shoes
made to walk the tightrope
they've been in a cupboard in Wales
for nearly 30 years

they were hand crafted in Tepoztlán, Mexico
for an artist in a women's circus
the closest thing to bare footedness
in soft well-fitted leather

the shoemaker from northern Mexico
a theatre man, poet, occasional cobbler
the circus acrobats and clown
jugglers and musicians

from east and west of the US and UK
lived a month in the village
then took their show to Nicaragua
1987, days of Sandinista Revolution

the budding tightrope walker
after some time
ceased to practise balancing over space
carefully put the shoes away

in the next millennium by chance
she meets the shoemaker poet in Sydney
he remembers the women's circus
reminds her, he made those shoes

Wish them new life
for here is a good rope
over years and miles
stretching

Love stories

My life in Mexico

Manon Saur

MANON SAUR is also known as Manon Saur (de la Fonteijne) de Vignal on her documents. She married a Mexican diplomat (who served in Australia) and lived in Mexico from 1989 to 1991. She represented Mexico in France, Sweden and Poland for the following eight years with frequent visits to Mexico. She studied art at the Brisbane Technical College which eventually became the Queensland College of Art – Griffith University. With four children and a busy social calendar, there was not a lot of time to pursue an artistic career. After the end of her marriage and when her children left for universities in Mexico and Australia, Manon stayed in Poland and pursued her own career, painting again and teaching business English as a second language in Polish companies. She developed *Studio Marmalada* in Warsaw, a large creative space where she held her own exhibitions and collaborated with other artists. Manon now lives on the south coast of New South Wales in Australia where she still spends time painting and exhibiting work. Her children and grandchildren are not far away and, thanks to modern technology, she continues to have contact with her two adopted daughters in Mexico. She has no experience in writing, but feels a book inside. Who knows what the future may bring.

It was 1989 and arriving in Mexico was a culmination of choices which in retrospect amounted to only one choice: to be with the man I loved. A man with two children, who had vowed to take care of my two children and to whom I had made a similar vow to take care of his. Together we would take on the world.

I had no idea what it would all mean.

I didn't even speak Spanish and neither did my children. Even worse, the best choice of school for us was the French Lycée. I didn't speak French either and neither did my children. His children, even though they were still very small, did speak both languages. They had attended the French school in Canberra and had grown up with a father who had always spoken Spanish with them.

My husband had been a diplomat in Australia and was returning home to the Ministry of Foreign Affairs where he became Director General for Europe. One of his first missions shortly after we arrived in Mexico City was to fly to Davos, Switzerland, on a reconnaissance trip for the upcoming World Economic Forum, leaving me and the four children to assimilate.

I don't even want to dwell on the apartment we first inhabited except that, from time to time, I had to climb onto the roof and pull some wires out of the *tinaco*, a holding tank for the water supply which emptied for lack of pressure. This action allowed it to fill again. It always seemed to happen when it was shower time for the kids and I was terrified of heights. I was watched with great interest by the others in the building... this *gringa* from 'who knows where'.

Eventually, we were to have a driver but until that time, my sister-in-law offered me a car to go shopping (for groceries) and to pick the children up from school. The deal was that I picked up her FOUR children also. That's eight children! Needless to say, it was impossible to use safety belts!

One has to know what the *Lyceo Franco Mexicano* looks like at 2.00pm when school's out. The main entrance was on the corner of Homero and Av. F.C. de Cuernavaca, which was totally grid-locked in a traffic jam with cars and drivers waiting to pick up children pouring out of the doors; about two thousand, from kindergarten age to teenagers sitting for their baccalaureate. It was jaw dropping! One by one mine would saunter out, only to be drawn like magnets to the street vendor on the corner selling snakes, *tarántulas* and scorpions. More than once I left the car in the middle of the street to cross the road and guide them back to the parked car. Lessons were taught in French and, in the playground, they had to speak Spanish. Learning two languages at once was heavy duty for my two children aged ten and six, but all the changes in our lives were just as hard for my adopted girls, aged six and five.

I was thrown into a similar situation when I arrived with my parents in Australia in 1960 from The Netherlands without speaking a word of English so I had some knowledge of what they were going through. There was a lot of crying but there was more laughing. It was fun and every day we were confronted by the surreal essence of Mexico.

Soon (and not soon enough) my husband returned from Davos. He was away for two weeks during which time I made some major decisions by myself, which included choosing our new home.

We moved into the house and our stuff arrived from Australia. Everyone was very excited. With familiar things around us, we finally fell into some kind of routine. The garden of our house was not a big one, but surrounded by gum trees which made me feel at home. A *barranca* bordered our garden and gum trees were all we could see from our windows. The house was modest, spacious, light and bright, and situated in the Huizachal, a military enclave, not far from Tecamachalco. Because of the terrible pollution in the city even then, I made a big fuss about having air purifiers in every room, every bedroom. We used them for a week I think and then forgot about them. As soon as we walked in our front door, the sight of the trees outside and the open spaced, light filled rooms made it feel like an oasis; tranquil and cool, when the temperatures outside were hot and stifling.

I had brought a large trampoline from Australia which turned out to be a 'to go to' place in good times and bad. It was a cubby house, a picnic blanket, a stage for theatre (the kids loved dressing up), a chat room or just for jumping on as children do.

Then my husband had to leave again and I was not quite ready to be a single mother in this unfamiliar place, but there were no choices. Just for a couple of weeks. The hot water suddenly disappeared and the toilets would not flush. My sister-in-law phoned the landlord who promised to resolve the problems *mañana*, however, after three days it was still *mañana*. It was unbearable. I insisted the landlord should come and look at the situation, which he did. I was ready with children, towels, shampoo and clean clothes and told him to take us to his house. Actually, I don't quite know what I said, but he got the point. He took us and we all had long showers and I made sure I had the longest of all. The problem was fixed the next day... and with smiles; people always seemed to smile in Mexico.

The business rhythm in Mexico is different to Australia and people usually started work late and finished late. My husband was a conscientious man and he left early in the morning with the children and dropped them at school. Lunch for him started at 3.00pm and finished at 5.00pm, at which time he could be back in the office until any hour; 10.00pm or later would not be unusual. However, he was the Director General for Europe, which was a position entailing lots of socialising and I was required to accompany him. Nearly every night there was a function organised by one of the ambassadors of the European Union; a cocktail, a concert with a cocktail, an opening of an exhibition and a cocktail, or a dinner. From most of these events one could usually escape reasonably early, but the dinners were formal. According to protocol, one could leave about 45 minutes after coffee and liqueurs were served. The three course (or more) dinner with speeches had a rhythm of its own. We were rarely back home before midnight. And then the next day it would start all over again. I was definitely sleep deprived in those days.

My wardrobe coped as I soon discovered the wonders of accessories on basic black. It always worked. I became obsessed with comfortable but still stylish shoes and made sure the heels were never worn. It didn't matter as I was an accessory myself dangling of the arm of the main guest.

We now had a *muchacha* (a girl who helped in the household), a driver, a car and I had made a friend. Magdalena was tall, with blond hair like Lady Godiva, an artificial tan and she had lots of children too. She was Italian married to an Italian diplomat. They had a big house in Tecamachalco with a pool and we spent many happy weekends with them.

Magdalena and I liked looking for out-of-the-way *mercados* to shop for vegetables and food. It was a deep desire of us to find the authentic Mexico and not walk the same path as every expatriate or tourist. We would park the car and as soon as we did, the car would be surrounded by young boys who wanted to carry our bags. All pushing and shoving; 'pick me,' they would cry and always be very polite. Which one to pick? The strong looking big one or the scrawny looking eight year old? As unfair as it may sound, I often chose the littlest one and oh, he would be so proud. He would take the task very seriously and the moment a purchase was made, he would make it his business to take control of the item, place it in the bag and off we'd trot.

'*Hola güeritas*' (hi blondies) was the sing song which greeted us from the vendors who yelled out with big smiles; 'come to my stall!' We definitely were the only blondies in a radius of many kilometres. But one day, I was standing at a stall selling delicious cream. There were big containers of different cream and the vendor would dip a small, crisp tortilla for us to try. And another and another. The creams tasted different as to the degree to which they were cultured from mild to sour cream. On this particular day, a woman with very dark skin stood next to me and the vendor said '*hola güerita*' to her and they both started laughing so we all had a big laugh. No doubt she was a regular customer... like we were.

Coming from a country like Australia where time is money and money is a high priority, I was always fascinated by the humble and generous attitude of people who came into our daily domestic life and who worked very hard for little money. There were not enough power points in the house for the televisions, computers, videos, cassette/CD players, printers, satellite dish, hair rollers, hair dryers, Nintendo, etc. so, we looked for an electrician. He came and he made giant holes in the walls which shocked me at the time. In no time at all, however, it was all patched and invisible and it was lucky that the walls were painted white and not some exotic colour which needed to be matched.

The electrician had an audience as the children were back from school and when the job was done, the man spent a long time weaving a scorpion from the copper wire stripped from an electrical cable. It was beautiful. As soon as he finished and gave it to one of the enthralled children, another clamoured to have one also. He patiently made four. One for each child; from the coarsest wire to a tiny one made of the very finest.

My husband, being Mexican, was at home in Mexico, unlike myself, being in a totally foreign environment. He had both family and friends as he was born and went to school in Mexico City. They represented a completely different circle of society. It was said that ninety percent of the wealth was owned by ten percent of the population and I don't imagine that a lot has changed. We spent our weekends in magnificent homes in Polanco and Coyoacán, and a little further in Valle de Bravo, about 160 kilometres from Mexico City, where a family member owned a home.

Apart from a few exceptions, the meetings with friends and family were probably the most difficult for me. Dinners went on forever; meals were served very late. The conversations were mostly political and my level of Spanish was hardly up to scratch to understand all of the double meanings in jokes, innuendos and the shared knowledge that only happens when people know each other well. I was just there ... and thank God I was blonde, otherwise I might have been invisible.

I really liked entertaining but being the hostess of reciprocal dinners was even more challenging as the guest of honour (and there was always a guest of honour) would often not appear until 10.00 pm or later and nothing could really start until then; except for a lot of drinking. There was help in the kitchen but to create a dinner for six, eight, twelve or more people, in an instant, and freshly cooked, that was a juggle. You never really knew how many people would turn up; how many extras.

Position and power mean a lot everywhere, but perhaps a little more in Mexico when so few have it. When it came close to Christmas time, there were daily deliveries of gifts; wine, baskets of conserved fruit, chocolates and all sorts of decorative things from Mexico, and signature touristic things from other countries as well. Mexico excels in all sorts of wonderful crafts; textiles, pottery, embroidery, painted boxes and trays, among other things.

Before Christmas time, at the end of October and beginning of November, there is *el día de los muertos* – the day of the dead. All Saints is celebrated around the world mostly as Halloween. In Mexico, this is celebrated in an incredible way and they have quite a unique relationship with death as it is seen as part of life. People visit graves, pray for the dead and honour the saints in Christian history. It's an elaborate happening in this country coupled with lots of humour. It is melancholic and while humour is inevitable, it does not make light of the loss felt when someone departs this earthly domain. From mid-October, the *mercado*s are filled with all kinds of Halloween paraphernalia, but by far the most noted and outstanding are the skeletons. They are pictured to perform the tasks of everyday life; dancing, marrying, singing, getting drunk and making love.

The skeletons are made out of papier-mâché or carved from wood, painted and decorated. They are small and large, and no matter how confronting, one cannot help but admire and have a giggle. (Google – skeletons Mexico – and you'll see what I mean.) Bread shops make loaves of bread in the shape of skulls and crossbones, and there are also beautifully decorated skulls made entirely of sugar, which are very colourful indeed. They have names on their foreheads; yours or for someone you may wish to surprise.

At home there is always an altar decorated with orange flowers – marigolds. With photos of parents and close relatives who have passed away. The altar is loaded with grains and perhaps a favourite dish of the dear departed and even some tequila or beer. Maybe even a *molcajete* (the traditional Mexican version of pestle and mortar) or a *metate*, a stone tool used to grind the corn for tortillas, the daily bread. There will also be many candles, skeletons and *papel picado* (thin perforated and colourful paper), hung up a bit like bunting. Everyone goes to the cemeteries and the most famous is the Pantheon San Andres Mixquic. We went with the whole family and were nearly crushed in the throng making its way down the main street to where people sit by the decorated grave sites, singing, eating, drinking and remembering their loved ones.

The *mariachis*, groups of musicians who sing and serenade, are ever present. They circle the grave site, wearing their suits adorned with silver and their well-known stylish *sombreros*, playing their violins, trumpets and guitars. Usually there are many such groups, often side by side, and the cacophony is quite deafening, unless you are lucky enough to be serenaded in the middle of such a group. After a while in Mexico you realise that everyone can sing with a great voice, and that everyone knows the words of every song.

In December (traditionally on the 16th) the *posadas* begin, a kind of re-enactment of Mary and Joseph searching for lodgings in Bethlehem. There are great processions in the Spanish-speaking world, a very famous one in Oaxaca, one of the most beautiful cities in Mexico. The celebration dates back to tenth or eleventh century Europe, where it was used to teach religious doctrine and was eventually banned by the church. The *posadas* were reinvented by the Spanish missionaries.

Now in Mexico, there are many parties with eating, drinking and singing, where half the guests are invited to go outside and take the roles of Mary and Joseph, singing something like 'let us in' and the others are inside, taking the role of the inn keeper, singing 'we have no place for you...' Then there is the breaking of the *piñata!* The *piñata* is a round clay pot wrapped in papier-mâché with seven points representing the seven sins. It is filled with vegetable, fruit and lollies. Then it's hoisted on a rope and the children (or adults), blindfolded, take turns in swinging at it with a stick. The stick represents faith or love.

Breaking it represents hitting the devil and making him let go of all the good things he has stolen.

We had arrived in Mexico in late October, so to be invited to a *posada* was one of our first experiences. There was a line of kids, who waited their turn to be blindfolded and then grabbed hold of a bat and tried to hit the *piñata*, which was moved by others from side to side to make it as difficult as possible. While this was happening, they would sing: '*dale, dale, dale............ no pierdas el tino*' – meaning 'hit, hit, hit, don't lose the knack'. My son's name is Dale, which is quite difficult for a Spanish speaker to say and, when asked how it was spelled, well... his nickname became *Piñata* in a blink of an eye. When the *piñata* is finally broken by the big guys who have been doing it for years, all the kids dive for the lollies and fruits which spill all over the floor.

Time went by. We were settling in and the children were beginning to relax, to speak the language and we were invited to many parties. Official duties were taking my husband here and there. I was on call to do things with the wives of diplomats and the International Women's Group (IWG). We also had great lunches with the whole family. There were plenty of wonderful places like the *Taquería Los Cocuyos*; one of our favourites was *Sanborns de los Azulejos*.

I had studied printmaking and painting but had not practised for quite a while. Life had been so hectic, but now I was ready to get back into it as all that creation around me was quite an inspiration. I bought an easel and started painting. I found someone who made frames already stretched with canvas which was great as in Australia I had made my own. There was no time to organise an exhibition, but at least I was painting whenever I could.

The *Club Reforma* was often a highlight on the weekends, usually during the winter, as in the summer months the rains would start falling around midday and then it became quite chilly. There were swimming pools and plenty of space to run free. Great for adults and kids. We found one of our cats there which was a little story. The adults were having a nice time, eating a bit, drinking a bit. It was always so relaxing to go there, sitting in the sun, reading a book or chatting about nothing important. Suddenly we were surrounded by wet children holding tiny little kittens which smelled horribly of petrol. The poor little things had no chance was my first thought. There was no doubt at all that the future planned for those little creatures was not good.

'Oh Mama... can we take them home???'

'No darling! We already have a cat!'

I tried hard to keep my distance emotionally as we really didn't need three more kittens. Upon the mention of petrol, the little band decided to take them into the showers and wash them. After a good scrubbing they brought them back for me to scrutinise but no, there was still a strong smell of petrol. 'Can we? Can we...?'

Off they went to do it again and again. It's not that I felt proud of myself for leaving this all in the hands of six and seven year olds, but what to do? The thought of an 'accidental' drowning did cross my mind, but what were the choices? The little band came back and thrust another creature under my noise. By this time some of the other parents had become involved and decided each to take one home, which left one poor little meowing kitten to face the world alone.

'Pleeeeeeaase???'

We took him home and he was named Sushi after one of our favourite gastronomic delights, very popular in Mexico where there is a large community of Japanese people. He was grey and white and grew to be very large cat with the thickest and longest fur; a testimony to petrol and soap. Sushi ended up traveling the world with us and lived in another three countries before making it back to Mexico where he died of old age.

It took a while to become deeply aware of the beauty of Mexico City. There are so many people and there seemed to be no order at all. There were half-built buildings of cement blocks with steel wires sticking out all over the place and gnarled knots of electricity wires bunched on ceilings and walls. Then right next to such a mess would be a beautiful 16th century church and glamorous modern buildings.

It was difficult to appreciate the city at first as your eyes tried to focus and were disturbed by the incongruity of the sights, the noise of cars and music and yelling street vendors pushing their carts and selling their wares. The traffic of six lanes going one way (and how would you find your way back), stray dogs and cats, people sitting and standing in doorways with no visible purpose and all the while, I was conscious of my handbag because I had been warned so many times to be vigilant. There were expensive cars which glided through the streets and avenues to their destinations amidst the chaos of humanity. A car would stop, a driver would jump out to open the door for magnificently-clad people, with manicured nails, coiffed hair and very clean shoes. Sometimes I was one of them and sometimes I would observe. I tried to be everywhere.

Mexico is a country of great contrasts and excesses. Of beauty, of music, art, craft and of joy. If you have fortune, you are obliged to take care of the less fortunate. When you hear a special whistle and find the man pulling a cart, who sharpens the scissors and knives, the knives get sharpened whether they need it or not. The house-keeping money given to the *muchacha* to buy tortillas and food for lunch or dinner is never accounted for. If her family from the village needs a place to stay, they will stay in your kitchen or her room, or wherever, somewhere; invisible... just don't ask and don't see. If she's honest, you are blessed. She's another member of the family and her family in need is your family.

My sister-in-law came home late one weekend from Valle de Bravo to find that her newly employed *muchacha* had just given birth to a baby, all by herself, alone in her room. Nothing had been noticed or said so it was quite a shock. So it was off to the local *supermercado* called Gigante late in the evening to buy nappies, clothes, and whatever else was necessary for a newborn. Another member of the family!

For me, Mexico was a whirlwind. Surrealistic in every way. I was thrown into a life of sudden motherhood for four in a strange country. This entailed supporting them in adjusting to each other and the changes, when I was barely coping with adjusting myself. Then my husband became Chief of Protocol and life notched-up into an even higher gear. Almost daily, events lurched from domesticity to glamorous events where I would meet heads of state and great figures in politics, literature, and the arts, and where I learned how to stand still for long periods, go without lavatory stops, hold my hands in a certain way and keep opinions to myself.

For days, we travelled with Lee Kuan Yew and his entourage to Acapulco and then to Cancún on ancient presidential planes. I don't like flying and there were moments when I didn't think we'd make it back when passing through a storm. We did of course!

Another highlight was a trip we made to Los Mochis and beyond by train; the Chihuahua al Pacífico, leaving from Chihuahua. This turned to be another example of, in Mexico, it matters who you know, not what you know. Researching the train schedules to Chihuahua from Mexico City, it appeared that there was no passenger train going that way. Just goods trains. My doubts grew by the minute. But, my husband knew a man who knew a man in the railways and he came home excited and announced that they were going to add a passenger wagon to the goods train for the trip and I thought that the demand for this journey must have increased. It was a 30-hour trip from Mexico City to Chihuahua and I was not very excited to do this with four children without beds to sleep in. I was imagining the whinging about the discomfort, not to mention my own but we went anyway. Taking masses of sandwiches and great bottles of water was a good idea I thought. The train was leaving at 6.00pm and we arrived at the station some time before that. I was surprised that the driver could take us very close to the train. The end carriage was the first carriage and the closest to us and in front of the entrance of the carriage was a welcome committee of four men. No idea who they were, but each one was introduced and one presented me with flowers. The water and sandwiches, with our bags and belongings, were whisked away and we were ushered into the train. The carriage was to be ours alone. Inside was a sitting room, a dining room, two bedrooms, a bathroom and a kitchen where I never ventured. We were introduced to our chef, valet, waiter, engineer(?) and the man who supervised it all. There was a little balcony at the back of the train where we could sit and see where we had been... endless hours of train tracks... it was hypnotizing with many photos taken of tunnels we had just passed through.

The train pulled out of the station and we were invited to the dining room where the table was set with crystal and porcelain, and dinner was served. It was stunning, and we never saw the sandwiches again. This started our trip which lasted almost three weeks. The next morning the chef asked each one of us what we'd like for breakfast and I was amazed how quickly the children responded. *Huevos rancheros, chilaquiles, huevos a la mexicana, huevos divorciados.* Hot cakes?... *Con un cafecito?*

Why the engineer? Well, when the train pulled into the next station, we had a choice: stay or continue. If we wanted to stay, the whole train would pull out of the station a small distance, then reverse onto another track, our carriage would be decoupled (by the engineer) and we could stay in the carriage, discover the town and continue the next evening when the next train came in on schedule. The train would be shuttled back and forth so our carriage would be coupled (by the engineer). Amazing. And so we continued to Chihuahua, coupling to the *Chihuahua al Pacífico* and on to Los Mochis while eating, lounging, sleeping, playing cards, cocktails at five, reading, eating again, drinking and just watching the passing country side which became spectacular on the way to the coast. No wonder it's a famous railway trip.

It ended up a very adventurous trip. From Los Mochis we travelled a little further north to Club Med for a week. I came down with Rubella (German measles). And while I felt I was dying in my hot room without air-conditioning, the rest of the family were diving, boating and having lots of fun. The Management of Club Med weren't keen for me to leave my room either. How did that happen that I was so unlucky? Who knows! The rest of the family did not catch it.

Our little palace on railway tracks was waiting in Los Mochis and soon we were on our way again and this time south to Guadalajara. One day, the train stopped and didn't move again for hours. The news finally came to us that because of heavy rain part of a bridge had collapsed. The train was stuck. We ended up taking a bus to Puerto Vallarta; a local bus with local people with baskets and chickens, and non-stop radio Salsa. After a few days in a mega hotel we were happy to hear that the train was able to get through, although sadly two people lost their lives repairing the bridge. We joined the train again in Guadalajara after seeing the sights of this magnificent city and especially the murals of José Clemente Orozco. And then back to Mexico DF. It was a never to be repeated experience and we were so privileged.

We fell in love with Mexico and just as we were all really settled in and the strange was no longer strange, we were sent to a post in Paris. That was also very exciting but we were very sad to leave our life in Mexico and all the friends we had made. Every year, we looked forward to returning to Mexico. By my husband's side, I represented Mexico for nearly ten years. I tried to be as Mexican as I could by organising dinners with Mexican food and dressing up in a *charro* suit on one or two national days but I would always be a *gringa*. We picked *huitlacoche* (also known as corn smut or Mexican truffle), a fungus which grows on corn, in a corn field in Stockholm. It is quite a toxic fungus unless it's gone through a cooking process and only Mexicans eat it, as far as I know. It's an acquired taste and when cooked with garlic and put in a pancake, it's delicious. The Aztecs called *huitlacoche* black gold. That cornfield in Stockholm had been punished by so much rain that the blight was everywhere. The farmer let us pick baskets full and could not imagine why we wanted it. He is still laughing and telling the story I suppose.

So, as diplomats, we spread the word about this wonderful country, its people, the culture and the amazing cuisine. Many fruits and vegetables originally came from this part of the world: *cacao* for chocolate, tomatoes, the many varieties of chilies, vanilla, avocado and corn, to name just a few, all came from Mexico. There is so much more and there are fruits which are still not known by the wider world.

My marriage did not last and eventually my two step-daughters moved to Mexico to attend university. We have regular contact and I will always feel like their mother. The split was devastating at the time and my children moved back to Australia where they also continued their studies at university. The bond continues and my daughter has travelled to Mexico several times to see her step-sisters. I hope that one day they'll be able to come to Australia so I can meet their children and we can all sit around the table once again.

Until then, a piece of my heart will always be in Mexico.

Magical

Jacqueline Buswell

you might be blessed or cursed when visiting
sub-tropical Catemaco, a town by a lake
with an island where monkeys rule

the land is made of old volcanoes
those growing up here know a wealth
of springs creeks mountains forests

plants birds animals
and have to learn the rest
of the world is poorer

the people are ancient as the Olmecs
their knowledge ranges from primeval
to contemporary

the lake-side farm is deep green on dark loam
homes are humble, domestic fowl abundant

we buy eggs honey cheese
and talk of medicinal properties of plants
looking all the while for the local shaman

the region is famous for its *brujos*
who might put a spell on you

Camino de flores

Rachael Byrne

RACHAEL BYRNE is an experienced producer with a demonstrated history of working in creative industries. Rachael obtained her Bachelor of Arts in film, French and English from the University of Sydney and also studied at McGill University, Montreal. Upon completing her studies, Rachael began working in film and advertising, a career which has given her extensive experience across live action, animated and digital projects. Her film experience includes *The Office Mug* (2010), *Happy Feet 2* (2011), *The Lego Movie* (2014), *The Inksect* (2016), *Como Filmar Una XXX* (2016) and the animated TV Series, *Lukas Storyteller* (2019). In 2013, Rachael moved to Mexico City to form part of the founding team of MaliArts, an animation and post-production studio. Since then, Rachael has led production at MaliArts, growing its body of work to include diverse creative projects with Mexican and international clients across film, television and advertising.

I was late to the game to read 'Eat Pray Love', and was struck recently when I finally did, to see that over five years, I accomplished what Elizabeth Gilbert set out to do in the Italy part of 'Eat Pray Love' and what I think many people are inspired to do at some point in their life. Completely immerse yourself in another culture, especially a culture as beautiful as Mexico. I don't know anyone that hasn't come here once and, upon leaving, immediately mentally planned their next trip. A saleswoman in Sydney I was communicating with to organise for my Mum to collect a quilt for me to bring over on her next visit (and so goes the expat life) said – when I wrote I was in Mexico – 'Oh Mexico. I travelled there last year, and I cannot wait to go back. To explore

Monte Alban this time'... and so goes the first-time visitor to Mexico. There's too many treasures and it's too much fun.

In grocery stores in Mexico, senior citizens pack your groceries for you and custom is you tip them. I love this tradition, because I've never seen a lovely older man or woman miserable with this post. There's banter, joking, laughing and some serious packing going on! I just had an amazing laugh with a man at the store near work and these are the moments when I realise, I did it. Making a local joke equates to dreaming in another language, true understanding (even if your past tense conjugations are legions away from perfect, as likely, they always will be).

Mexico is a truly surreal and magical country. André Breton, when he landed here, said he'd never felt anything so surreal. I think that's why people are so curious to visit. At the surface there is the fiesta, which we all love, and if you are traveling here in a small town is a must do. Deeper though there is something ethereal about Mexico.

When García Márquez won the Nobel Prize, he spoke of Latin America's tribulations as a 'source of insatiable creativity, full of sorrow and beauty, all of which this roving and nostalgic Colombian is but one cipher more, singled out by fortune. Poets and beggars, musicians and prophets, warriors and scoundrels, all creatures of that unbridled reality, we have had to ask but little of imagination, for our crucial problem has been a lack of conventional means to render our lives believable.' That couldn't sum it up better, rendering the everyday believable.

My father-in-law gave me a pendant, well he held out five pieces of jewellery and I had to choose which one was for me. The pieces came from the pyramids hidden in the mountains of Malinalco, little Obsidian pieces hand carved by the Aztecs and left there when they were wiped out by Spanish stomach flu. Jorge told me to carefully consider which I wanted and indeed one little one caught my eye and my hand reached for it. I wore this piece all the time, I just loved that it was from 'sometime before 1500'. It was the emblem of the god of the wind, Ehécatl, a beautiful god next to my favourite called Tlaloc. Innocent enough, however, after some time we were sleeping in Malinalco, at my parents-in-law's house from where you can see the pyramids. I had a terrible night. Awful nightmares, horrific, bloody and brutal! Long and short, I butchered and cooked some people in a gigantic *pozole cazuela*, after which I snapped up property in Sydney that someone in the group was vying for. It's the perfect combination of two horrible things, carnivorous Aztec Mexico and well, the carnivorous Sydney property market.

I came down to breakfast, too weirded out by my nightmare and fitful night to share it and told everyone I slept well. After several coffees and hours at the table chatting, which remains just the best thing to do at my parents-in-law's house, I confessed my terrible night with my terrible dreams. They all laughed at me, and then immediately my mother-in-law fished the pendant off from around my neck and said '*mejor no*'. Best not. My mother-in-law is wonderfully matter of fact. She explained it needed a *limpia*, a clean by which it's left out under the moonlight for a full cycle of the moon. So, she hung it on their rooftop by the cactus and it was returned to me a full moon later. Job done, I never had this dream again. It doesn't matter if it's true, if it worked or not, if it beggars belief, this country is undeniably magical.

Then there are the constant blessings, rituals and continual ceremony. We are building a house in Malinalco and the process has been as follows. First the seller was found and the deal was made, deed signed and witnessed by a public notary. After spending a year conceptualising the house between us and my architect father-in-law, we broke land and the ceremony began. First, just us and my parents-in-law went to the land with rose quartz, gold coins and copal incense. We stood and faced north, south, east and west. Asking permission at each turn. Then the sky, the moon, the sun and then leaning down we touched the earth. Then Pablo and I had to bury the quartz and coins at four points under where our house now sits. We had to speak of our intention to the land. All this while the copal was burning beautifully and wafting around the site. After all this, I walked up to our car and a family had stopped and was walking towards the entrance, waving at us. I asked my mother-in-law if she knew them and she said she didn't, but as they walked down the hill her face lit up and she went to them. Indeed, she knew them, it was the *Señora* we had bought the land from. With her long plaits, beautiful *rebozo* around her shoulders, her children and her grandchildren; three generations just happening to pass by this remote country road our house is on. She was so happy to hear we were doing the ceremony and of course gave us her full blessing in the form of a big warm hug.

Pablo then had his wisdom teeth taken out and, per dentists here, I was promptly given them in a box by the surgeon soon as he'd finished. Not sure what to do with them, the obvious answer came from Malinalco, you bury them in the land, it's tradition. So somewhere under the foundations with the rose quartz and gold coins are Pablo's wisdom teeth. But it would not be complete if we hadn't then buried four horse shoes from a mare at the four corners of the house. So that all came together after my mother-in-law put the call out around town for four horse hooves. Then, we turned the first sod, with a bottle of French and old friends from home. Nailed it.

I think it's my parents whom I can thank for giving me the curiosity to live here. When I was just 16, they sent me to stay with Great Uncle Barry, who despite his name had left Australia in the 1940's and established himself in Paris as a man more French than a Frenchman. Barry, with his cashmere sweaters, cravat and impeccably pressed shirts. Barry who took me everywhere, stopping by at his favourite cafe for a noisette and chat with the barista. Barry who took me for my first glass of champagne at the Moulin Rouge, tours of Paris by night, showing me the ropes of the metro and then leaving me alone to navigate the city, independent and just 16. I loved it. If we went somewhere together, Barry would have planned the whole day. If I needed to buy some jeans – perfect, we'll shop at the Opera with his partner Blandine and we'll walk to Hotel Crillon for *le menu* when we're done. If I went somewhere alone, we'd sit in his apartment at the end of the day when I returned and he'd make me explain my day in French. Up to what metro lines I took, where I changed stations, what I ate, where I stopped. It was fabulous, although I'm now embarrassed to admit I never told him about the McDonald cheeseburgers I'd sneak in before dinner.

Over the years my trips to Paris would always be marked by a day and a *coupe de champagne* with Barry, until our last with my husband on our honeymoon, which I didn't know at the time, would actually be our last. Blandine called me last year with the news Barry had peacefully passed away. I like to think Barry knows his fabulous tour legacy lives on here, where I mentally plan tours around the city with visitors, only swapping the coupe for a copa de mezcal.

We have had a constant stream of visitors from all over and, before they arrive, off I go around the city planning what to do. We may spend some time wandering through Chapultepec, stopping by the cave where they play classical music on a Sunday to a silent crowd on benches leaning back, we head down to Juárez and find our way through all the old mechanic workshops to the best gelato I've ever had, olive oil flavour being their speciality. Continue on downtown and go up to the dated Torre Latino for a *michelada* pointing out the surrounding mountains and not just one but two, often snow-capped, volcanoes. Pop into a *cantina* for some *pimientos de padrones* and a fine *tequila* with its *sangrita*. Without a doubt along the way there will be music, poetry, maybe a protest, and so it goes in Mexico.

Of course amongst all our visitors there are plenty of Australians, which can go either way to be honest. One such Australian told me over a glass of wine they could not bring their Mum to Mexico because she is racist and only likes high-end. What an unbelievable thing to say. I was driving with another Australian friend and looking out the window we saw some kids selling things at the traffic lights, they said, 'aren't we lucky we weren't born here'. Again, what a statement, I know plenty of people happy to be born here. Sadly, although she had no bad intentions, that was the limit of her experience here. I miss my country and Australians dearly, and I imagine we'll live between there and here for the rest of our lives, cultural diplomacy doesn't come naturally to my people though.

Back to those five years ago, pre-Mexico, my partner had accepted a position at Pixar Vancouver, I was going to do my MBA and learn Spanish in VC. After which, me being a planner, all going well we would move to Mexico, open our business. Pixar Vancouver closed so suddenly our boxes were still somewhere on the Pacific and we were still in Mexico waiting for Canadian immigration papers to arrive. Being more bureaucratic than the film *Brazil*, five years later we are still in a sense at it with the paperwork and not all the boxes have arrived. That's ok. With no planning and zero notice, we did launch our business, I've scrambled the Spanish together, survived a scorpion sting. We were married, been through a major earthquake and since day one, I'm grateful for Pixar closing. Out of nowhere I had been flung out of my world, suddenly finding myself living in Mexico.

As awful as experiencing an earthquake is, what followed afterwards was the most awe-inspiring display of community. It hit just before lunch on, inexplicably, the same day as the devastating one in 1985. Immediately sporadic volunteer centres opened up, we spent the day at one and hours in, there were human chains of people trucking in and out canned goods, water and medical supplies. Pablo was coordinating food, I was at the front gate directing bikes where to go after they had stocked up again with first aid and water. People were told not to drive so there would be no traffic for ambulances, so some streets were empty and, as you walked, big groups of people passed wearing hard hats, pickaxes on their shoulders, heading to wherever help was needed. These were normal people, who had normal jobs, who had joined the famous *brigadistas* that day. Same as the people on bikes, who spent the rest of the week tirelessly transporting goods around the city. Huge human chains formed in some neighbourhoods, loading up trucks and helping sort through donations. Real everyday heroes responding to an unspoken call to action.

Every day we walk past buildings that fell in 1985, still abandoned, and then the ones from 2017. It took me some time to realise that instead of reminding us of our fragility, they remind us of our resilience.

When we were packing for Vancouver, I'd sent everything I'd thought we could make a home with there. A friend gave me some orange and blue enamel cups with a jug, they went from Sydney to Vancouver in the boxes back in 2013. Then of course sent to Mexico from Vancouver, which took months and months. The boxes arrived one at a time, the first was exciting, until I opened it to find all my books soaked in water and my folder of recipes disintegrated; some were hand-written and scrawled on the back of brown paper bags at my favourite cafe in Sydney. The next box was full of shattered ceramics. How on earth did Pixar send these? By the time the box arrived with the cups and jug, I was so happy to see they were still solid and gorgeous. At least one thing was resilient, which was enough. But, two cups had stuck together. Five years later, after many house guests, dinner parties of people convinced they could get them apart... everyone had tried everything and it was accepted as impossible. Then the other week, we had a picnic, Sunday dinner guests and Monday dinner guests. It came up again, more ideas. Something ignited for Pablo, and so easily in just a few seconds they came apart. Nothing is impossible. Especially love. Especially following your heart when it takes you away from where you're from, with all the difficulties and adventures that come with that, and opens up new roads you never thought you'd walk on.

Little things of nothing

Jenny Pollak

FOR MOST OF HER LIFE JENNY has been a full-time artist, focusing her arts practice in photography, sculpture, and, more recently, video installation. For a period of ten years Jenny also performed as a percussionist, flautist and backing vocalist with various Latin American bands and, in 1987, toured Latin America with *Tumbalé*. Her musical career culminated in a performance at the opening ceremony of the 2000 Paralympic Games in Sydney with the contemporary Latin song group *Telares*. In 2012, while continuing to make art, Jenny began a dedicated poetry practice. She has since been shortlisted for various prizes and has won the WB Yeats Poetry Prize and the Bruce Dawe Poetry Prize. Her poetry has been published in *Cordite*, *Meanjin*, the *Australian Poetry Journal* and various anthologies, including *Australian Award Winning Writing 2017*. Her website can be found at: https://jennypollak.viewbook.com/.

BACK STORY

In 1984 in a tiny outdoor restaurant in Valdottavo, Italy, Jenny Pollak broke five wine glasses while drumming a fast rhythm with her cutlery as she waited for her pizza to arrive. In a moment of intoxication that had nothing to do with the wine the trajectory of her life changed forever. Three months later, and back in Sydney, Jenny began attending percussion workshops at *La Peña*, a Latin American Cultural Centre. It was here that she met Claudia Vidal with whom she went on to develop a close friendship. Claudia would often talk about her brother Luis, in Mexico City. As a fellow photographer Jenny greatly appreciated his black and white photographs hanging on the walls of Claudia's house. In 1988, knowing that he was going through a difficult moment in his struggle with Multiple Sclerosis, Jenny decided to send him a letter. She wrote to tell him that she was a close friend of his sister. She wrote to tell him that she loved his photographs and to cheer him on in a hard moment.

With no expectation that they would ever meet, or even that he would answer her letter, Jenny wrote with an openness and honesty that was the beginning of a correspondence that grew over the following year into a deep friendship and trust. Eight months into their correspondence Jenny and Luis simultaneously wrote each other a letter declaring their love.

Photo: *This sharing of the air* – Jenny Pollak.

Extracts from correspondence between Luis Vidal and Jenny Pollak, 1988-1989

Jenny Pollak

MARCH 1988, MEXICO CITY

Dear Jenny,

Through my window I see a beautiful line of enormous eucalypts that cover most of the view and make this place look as the valley of Mexico once was at the turn of the century. From the window I only see a beautiful spot that was once called *la región más transparente del aire*. 'The most transparent region in the air.' I must say I'm lucky having this view in front of my desk and right now a tempest is moving the trees and the clouds I'm seeing and it makes me happy.

It's a pleasure to know I haven't lost my English and can explain to you what's happening to me. As you'll be able to read, this is a truly egotistical letter and I hope that soon I'll have other things to talk about. I hope that soon I'll talk about Mexico City whose people I really long to see and be a part of, to cross looks with those who really look.

I once went last year in the subway and I was agreeably shocked by the way people from Mexico City look without hypocrisy. When they're mad they seem to have a shotgun in their eyes; lovers make love with the looks they give each other, and nobody seems to look

LOVE STORIES | EXTRACTS FROM CORRESPONDENCE BETWEEN LUIS VIDAL AND JENNY POLLAK, 1988-1989

'decently'. I should say people in Mexico City simply and naturally look without hiding it. They don't stare but you feel you exist.

I had a very agreeable surprise with this being used to the looks in France where people look at you so 'decently' you end up asking yourself if you're not becoming transparent or simply non-existent. And here in Mexico you can feel you exist with the looks of the others, and I'm waiting to go and join my look to this net of looks that is so important a part, for me, of this huge and terrible agglomeration that was once Mexico City.

APRIL 1988, SYDNEY

Dear Luis,

Here I sit attempting to construct a fragile link across the Pacific. It's a bit like making a picture and your letter in return like a painting. It's exciting to slowly build up a picture of a friend stroke by stroke in this way. I am impatient now that you join your look to this net of looks that exists in Mexico City. It is an image I would like to paint.

Here in Sydney lives seem to me to pass side by side rarely touching, a little like the feeling of being transparent that you describe in France. Perhaps that is why I felt such a strong sense to write to you. It is sad to live in a society one does not feel a part of, a commitment to, an involvement with, or a sense of reality about. One day I would like to have those things around me, but until then I will reach out for them where they are to be found...

My impetus to write to you came in a strange and indirect fashion from the sense of empathy I felt just hearing about you and seeing your photographs, but I don't know you yet and so I write intuitively, as I would for myself and hope that there is some kind of communication, some connection. Despite the blind nature of this correspondence it is a nice way to meet someone. I apologise if this letter sounds sentimental, I am feeling quite free to write impulsively what enters and passes through my head, and in some things I am sentimental – certainly as a photographer, though increasingly as an artist I am drawn to express my astonishment at the world...

MAY 1988, MEXICO CITY

Dear Jenny,

I'm enjoying writing this letter a lot and the beautiful singing of the birds and the music I love help me to enjoy it more so that maybe I'll end up sending you a manuscript for a book. I'm asking myself if I'll have the energy and discipline to write a book if I'm not able to continue making photos, I want to share my enjoyment of life and my indignation and wrath against all that's done against life and joy. I'm listening to a record of medieval and renaissance music called 'Música Iucunda' – a joyful music and one that helps me to keep on smiling.

Going back to the world after living for some years as an unable person, even if I was only partially unable and did lots of things, always I had a wheelchair in my mind, and still now there it lingers. And although I've been told by people I trust that this treatment I'm having has worked I won't really believe it until I start feeling it in me. It's still a five week thriller and I can tell you it thrills me more than any book or film.

Part of your letter, the part where you talk of the feeling of strangeness you have in Sydney and I've been having in Paris and Mexico City, sent me spinning for more than a while with these ideas: not being able to feel part of a society, nor feel commitment to, involvement with or a sense of reality about. I quote it because it is part of my decision to come to Mexico. I decided to return thinking that here it will be easier for me to answer these questions, for in Paris I longed for tortillas, I missed 'my' mountains and wanted, I still want, to photograph sixteenth century convents in Mexico, built in the first years of the conquest when the monks, at least a very important one, had under his arm Thomas More's 'Utopia', and built really sensuous convents.

I want to photograph all the richness I found in these severe and monastic buildings built before Rome installed its dominion in the new world. But all these thoughts have to be revised and constructed patiently because dreams don't exist if one doesn't build them oneself, and I know my dreams won't exist if they're not made by me, because none of what one talks about exists outside oneself and only love, so I think, can end one's solitude.

My siesta of Monday noon ended when a big urge to write about my photos awakened me. Now I have the firm intention of writing the text for a book of my photographs wanting it to be poetry. I think I have some photographic joys I can share as I will share a photo of 'my' eucalyptus. I can think of my photos as poems.

Watching these eucalyptus of mine during a tempest while listening to the music I love is such a joy that maybe I'm making an effort to stay here. I'm happy watching my giant eucalyptus that for me represents the once unpolluted, so I remember it, Valle de Mexico that I loved, and still love and long to see and wander in.

JUNE 1988, SYDNEY

Dear Luis,

Your letter arrived to my house overflowing with a vitality and strength I am coming to associate with you. It is not enough to sit down in a cosy chair and idly read through your lines, your words and images demand ones real presence, that you be there, that you plunge in and become part of their experience. So to get your letter is to have a small adventure, and I'm very happy for that, and for this weaving of threads that grows between us...

If I could choose a piece of music now it would be Bach's double violin concerto.

Some days later, and it is two in the morning and I'm having a 15 minute break from the mind-numbing job that I've been doing for three weeks. I am working from midnight to 7am cutting and packing negatives and photographs at a machine on a factory floor at Kodak, then I sleep during the daylight hours. The effect is disastrously more horrific than I imagined it would be. I feel as if my life is slipping away without my having lived any of it, and my most real moments come in sleep... while I work my mind does not belong to me and I can feel a big gloom spreading through me as the days pass, filling me with an apathy I don't have the strength to resist...

It's 4am and in the last two hours I have managed to sneak in two or three of my own thoughts between other peoples' babies, weddings, birthday parties and overseas trips. I'm sorry to drag you into my boredom but now that I have you here life is tolerable again. Although it's dark outside and the view from here obscure and uninteresting I know that soon the sun will come up and flood colour into the sky and I will be on my way home to my bed and my head will be mine again...

JULY 1988, SYDNEY

Hello again at four in the morning from this laminated cafeteria. I wanted to tell you about something real here amidst all the machinery that numbs my brain. I saw a photo (amongst the thousands of photos that pass through my hands each night), a photo of a young girl with glasses of about six or seven years of age. She was smiling, her smile shy and hopeful. Her smile was innocent and vulnerable and it caught me by surprise, stopped me in my tracks, for in it I saw my sister, my twin, at that age and I suddenly remembered how she used to look, used to be. So full of joy and wonder. And this photo showed me that she has lost something of the look she had – that part of her smile that came from unquestioning trust, her vulnerability showing itself. And that photo has made me sad for something of beauty that has been lost forever, for the losses we suffer in growing up, for something irreplaceable. Her smile was a wilderness and a rainforest and it hurts to discover that it is no longer there.

LOVE STORIES | EXTRACTS FROM CORRESPONDENCE BETWEEN LUIS VIDAL AND JENNY POLLAK, 1988-1989

I'm glad to write this down, to share this sadness with a friend, not to forget this feeling but to record a real moment before it has gone and is swamped by the hundreds of unreal moments that must pass. And although this was a moment of sadness it was intense and real inside this swamp of days that pass so tastelessly.

And now it is tonight and what I hear on the news makes me cry for the people of Palau in the Pacific who fight for freedom from ships carrying nuclear power to the American bases with whom they must share their land; for their loss of innocence, their betrayal, their corruption and their struggle. And I know it is for things like this that my sister's smile is incomplete.

Another few days have spun by, these with a glow that is coming back now that the depression of the night work starts to lift...

How are your eucalyptus trees and the sky that falls?

Bach's Musical Offering has just ended and the night is very quiet and cold.

AUGUST 1988, MEXICO CITY

Dear Jenny,

I'm hearing, one time and another, a cassette you sent that happens to be one of my favourite pieces of music: Marin Marais' *Sonneries de Ste. Genevieve du Mont*. I'm hearing that cassette knowing it was, I hope still is, your favourite with a joyful 'amazement'.

Some days later...

This moment I'm living right now is a very hard one and, in some ways, a great one.

I'm fighting against myself in order not to stay in the 'cosiness' of invalidity. Yesterday I was told of a horoscope that had been made for me and if the astrologist is serious my horoscope is great, and if he is not I'm planning to make him seem so. I'm a non-believer, a sceptic who believes in his own strange way. I'm a materialist who thinks that matter is one of the ways light appears to us, a materialist who cannot live without poetry and the mystery, alchemy I call it, of the ways men and women can make matter 'talk'. I once 'spent' a whole morning in London's National Gallery 'talking' with Rembrandt's paintings and I 'spend' hours 'talking' with the eucalyptus trees in front of my window...

SEPTEMBER 1988, MEXICO CITY

This has been a cosy, I'm home, grey and rainy week, the kind of weather this thirsty country needs; the green trees look great against the leaden sky and taking a good photo of these trees, my friends and companions, is one of the reasons I have for getting better. It is hard needing other people, even when loving them, to do the things you need, not being able to do the things you would like to do, which are in some ways the things you need more. I would love to work on my photos, staying in the darkroom for days enlarging photos.

Photography is for me in some way what his novel 'A la recherche du temps perdu', 'In search of lost time', was, I think, for Proust, a search for the reasons and consistencies of his own life, and my files of negatives are the refreshment of my memory, and when I'm looking for a negative I travel in my memory and even hard times come back as good memories, I have been able to find enjoyment even in my worst moments.

I'm trying to recall my really hard times, like this one, and I've always been able to find a flower in the mud. That doesn't mean I have always stayed out of the mud, I had before a very black way of seeing life but now somehow in my very reduced world; my house; doctor's consulting rooms; the city as seen from a car; and the very reduced number of people I see I've been able to take joy out of little nothingness's. It is a way of talking, like rays of sun in the house, a flower, *las pequeñas cositas de nada*[1] as I call them, food is one of them and I'm hungry.

---

[1] Little things of nothing.

LOVE STORIES | EXTRACTS FROM CORRESPONDENCE BETWEEN LUIS VIDAL AND JENNY POLLAK, 1988-1989

SEPTEMBER 1988, SYDNEY

Dear Luis,

How stupid it is that we must spend so many of our days or nights inside buildings working at seemingly inconsequential things when this real world is all about us.

I say this because I feel so alive here on the beach, walking on sand, sitting on rocks, tasting salt in the wind, feeling the enormousness of the world about me and unable to comprehend how I could forget this, forget what is real.

Looking for another page to write on some papers fly out of my bag and it scarcely seems important to chase them across the rocks. The queen's head on a stamp has blown in a rock pool – how strange she is in this place...

So many things your letter sparks off in me. The rumble of thunder outside the window has taken me back to my childhood and now I read your letter that has just arrived to my door (leaning there against the glass) where you talk of the nostalgia the weather brings you, and I had been sitting here with the window open letting in the cold just so that I could enjoy more my nostalgia. You talk of the 'cosiness' of invalidity just at a time I was recognising my own temptation to fall into that pleasant lure of apathy which weaves itself quietly around me like a web.

Looking out the window I see the sky, a dark thunderous blue lit up by the sunlight, the last rays, and I know that such moments of intensity as this one will never let you or I sink too deep into that 'cosiness'. Esas pequeñas cositas de nada – nuestras salvavidas.[2]

Like the smile of my sister revived and relived in the snapshot of a child of six.

That one little drop of water on our heads is enough to dispel all the numbness that accumulates there...

---

[2] Those little things of nothing – our life savers.

NOVEMBER 1988, MEXICO CITY

Dear Jenny,

After all the terribly rough moments there are in Bach's suites for unaccompanied cello, I'm finally hearing the sixth, right now for me the most intelligently optimistic piece of music. I would like to be a cello...

I'm holding strongly a *nuestros salvavidas, esas pequeñas cositas de nada* and I feel that soon I'll be able to go outside walking, my legs begin itching, I really long to walk, to drift in a city, to get lost so I can find myself again, this is my favourite game: wandering in the streets trying not to get lost. I am an urban animal who would love a city without cars or little of them, a city mainly for human beings. Life in Mexico City is being killed by cars more than anything else...

I have been living with both these letters, yours and mine, all this time enjoying every moment of them, I have not 'answered' the last page of your letter; I just have to hear a fork crashing with a dish, or reading food in your letter to get hungry.

I have just passed a beautiful moment watching light become darkness. That last light of day is for me a very dear one, so much so that I often wait until black darkness to put on electric lights. And so today I waited for darkness before lighting the lamp for writing to you.

I hear you so well that it is difficult to send you this letter because I feel you so near while writing to you, a nearness I have only felt with my closest friend in Paris... this closeness between us comes only through these papers, what we put in them, and I consider it something great: trust, and even blushing and taking very long before typing it.

Love.

It's amazing how careful I am with this word, but in order to really say what I'm feeling I need it. Maybe I will never see you but it doesn't matter, the trust we give each other can be called love even staying only in letters. I hope this won't bother you, I had to write it like that, I couldn't keep on writing otherwise...

LOVE STORIES | EXTRACTS FROM CORRESPONDENCE BETWEEN LUIS VIDAL AND JENNY POLLAK, 1988-1989

NOVEMBER 1988, SYDNEY

Dear Luis,

Another day, and I sit in some warm rays of sunshine that fall through my kitchen window, a small halo of sunlight in a gentle breeze. Falling across my page a wonderful translucent shadow. I write and my words travel through it. The bottle that throws this shadow my mother gave me yesterday knowing that I would like it. The bottle itself is ugly, but the shadow it throws is beautiful and mysterious. Behind me on the stove is the bubbling sound of rice boiling and all about me the bigger sound of the music I am listening to – a cassette of baroque music I have just recorded for you. And now as I listen it is a pleasure to know you will hear it and look out your window at your eucalypts and it will join the air in the valley of Mexico.

That makes the world seem a cosier place – this sharing of the air....

The music has stopped and left my thoughts in the clearness of the drops of rain falling on the leaves outside. I'm glad we both feel brave enough for these words that we share. Your blush was my blush, your day and half of hesitation my day and a half of hesitation; and I love that blush and that day and a half of hesitation...

FEBRUARY 1989, MEXICO CITY

Dearest and loved Jenny,

Our correspondence carries on. This letter won't be as long and calm as the preceding ones but you were not coming. I'll try to answer fast, clearly and lovingly your last letter so you can read me before coming. Our correspondence, as our relationship, has already changed.

I remember dearly the calm of it but I love you and also love the craziness of what is happening... in a way we both know we are embarking on a perilous journey in good, the best, company there is.

I'm still afraid of the journey but not of you...

Bach has a new meaning for me, his music is part of that link we have built. *Courante*, a dance, means running as we have done this last month...

JANUARY 1989, SYDNEY

Dearest Luis,

It is hard to trust in the reality of something made only in paper, but both of us at the end of this paper chain, this fragile link, are real, and this gives a solidity to that which seems so fragile. These words are as light as the paper we write on, but the hands that write them are heavy, warm, real... I don't know how far to go on paper before we meet, knowing that we must test this love with the fire of reality. There is so much I want to say to you that I can't bear to say with you not here next to me.

FEBRUARY 1989, MEXICO CITY

We have gone as far as words will take us, even if I'll continue writing until I can hold your hands and hug you.

Photo: Luis and Jenny, taken by Claudia Vidal. (Excerpts from *Little Things of Nothing*, a book of black and white still life photographs and text by Jenny Pollak and Luis Vidal, compiled and edited by Jenny Pollak.)

A green chilli sauce made from tomatoes

Jenny Pollak

who knew love
could find itself
in the dark

like velvety moles
could tie a knot blindfolded

was a white letterbox
(confidante and celebrant)

between two hemispheres
a square dark room

more serious
than chat

who knew
love

was a difficult smile
in the face of a long sentence

(a disease takes time to kill you in its own fashion)

15,000 kilometres
is nothing

who knew the road was never going
to be yellow

that we were magicians

from out of our hats
we conjured the same

Conejo blanco![1]

whatever we wrote was already
written   inside our bones

our skins quickened
beneath our bravado

fear was an aphrodisiac
we pulled up like silk

we made it a virtue

jumped from the window of our twin
heads

eyes wide shut
and foundered   on air

---

[1] White rabbit.

oxygen was thin at that altitude
even the volcanos didn't appear

everything was the blue of distance

azul azul
tiene que ser...[2]

Yes! we said
Yes!

This is what love looks like
when you know

nothing's for keeps

---

[2] blue blue / it has to be (blue) – from *Muerte sin fin*, by José Gorostiza.

Pilgrimages

Jeannie Lewis

JEANNIE LEWIS'S CV is not so much a case of 'what's she done?' as 'what hasn't she done?' She's played at festivals around Australia and the world; performed with symphony orchestras, jazz bands, dance companies and leading cartoonists; written, devised and performed drama on stage and on air; recorded albums and sung on film and television sound tracks. Her connection with Mexico began in 1948 (at the age of three) when her father returned from representing the teachers of Australia at a UNESCO conference in Mexico City. He brought home with him some Diego Rivera prints, as well as two 78 recordings of instrumental Mexican music!! Jesse Street, also on that delegation, gave her a book called *Mitla and Lupe*. Mexico had arrived at Kingsford. Her first actual trip was via Mexico City to perform at the First International Festival of Protest Song in Cuba in 1967. Since then she has lived and performed in Mexico on several occasions; for birthdays, weddings, solidarity concerts and also professionally; her most 'prestigious' of that category being at the Festival Cervantino 1987, which was the subject of a one hour special for SBS TV.

JIM COTTER is one of Australia's most established composers for theatre, dance and film, having worked with all of the major theatre companies as well as a variety of dance companies and youth theatre organisations. He was the resident composer for the Australian National Playwright's Conference for a decade and has toured both nationally and internationally with his music. He has written works for the National Gallery of Australia for a number of exhibitions and has published a number of writings on music. A freelance artist for most of his career, he taught at the Australian National University for a decade and has now returned to full time composing.

Pilgrimages was written by Jeannie Lewis and recorded in 1987 by the ABC for a Radio Helicon program on Latin America.
Music composed and performed by Jim Cotter (1987)
All music copyright Jim Cotter
Audio-editing – Jeremy Cook (2020)
Engineer – David Bates (1987)
The link for the music can be found at: https://bit.ly/35PDVgi

For Hector
Héctor Caicedo, 1949-1987

'PILGRIM: a wanderer, a traveller in foreign parts, a sojourner; a person who travels to a shrine or holy place.'
'PILGRIMAGE: a journey undertaken by a pilgrim; specifically, a journey to some distant place, sacred and venerable, undertaken for devotional purposes. Figuratively, the journey of human life, the period between birth and death.'

MACHU PICCHU

Machu Picchu – Great Peak.
Shrouded in mists and mystery of time and nature, jungle and
    conjecture.
Lost city of the Incas,
Astride your mountain saddle,
You survey from on high,
The valley where the Urubambu River
Rushes down from the *tierras frías*
To mingle her Andean silt
With her Mighty Amazon Mother.

What feats of strength and servitude
Raised these giant blocks of stone
To such majestic heights,
To create you here close to the sky,
In the cool rarefied air
Where you seem to hang
by the teeth of your terraces?

Did the jungle give herself as your protector
And with the silent Indians maintain your secret?
The Spanish did not violate your temples.

Were you the birthplace of the Inca Dynasty?
Or, as the terminus in the constellation of fortress towns
A refuge for Inca Kings in the Conquistador years,
Till penetrated, much later, by archaeological curiosity?

Or did you become
The hiding place, the House of the Chosen Women –
The sacrificial maidens, Virgins of the Sun?

Could your priests divine the intrigue
Your mysteries would arouse in years to come?
And would they hear us now, or consume our sacrifice
If we should give ourselves to their rhythms,
Joined in dance, beneath the Inca Sun?

'Music was bound up with the dance and the dance with religion; all forms of religious expression involved dancing. The dance itself included singing; it was part of the collective hypnotism. The songs were repeated endlessly, monotonously; the evolutions of the dancer, the ornaments and the furiously rapid movements robbed all of the onlookers of their self-possession and gave them a feeling that their needs – for which the dance was designed – had been supplied.'

(V. W. von Hagen, *The Ancient Sun Kingdoms of the Americas*, 1961)

FROM BOGOTÁ, COLOMBIA
From Sydney, Australia, we came – to Mexico City

To further our studies,
You, in economics,
me, in experimental voice.
To forget old loves, and find new ones
In this vast land, so rich in poverty and beauty, corruption and
    culture.
To attune our souls to Mexico's,
To explore her past,
The Pyramids of the Sun and Moon
At Teotihuacán, City of the Gods.
To visit the Museum of Anthropology
And try to understand the ancient kingdoms of the Mayans and the
    Aztecs
With their complex Pantheon of Gods –
Cult, ritual, ceremony.

To travel across the cultural bridges,
Through the mammoth murals of that mammoth man
Diego – dedications to his people;
From 'The Branding of the Indians'
To 'Zapata and his White Horse'
And beyond

To the present-day pyramid of peso seekers,
Who, with fists clenched, faces upturned, through the pollution of air
    and administration,
Beseech god and government
To withhold earthquakes, and control the external debt.

This city of almost comical contrasts – of high-walled mansions and
    garbage-dump dwellings;
food-to-go, from Kentucky Fried, or taco street-vendors.

Perfumes of petroleum, tuba rose, corn-flour, and chile.
Corridos of revolutionary romance to fire the spirit,
Sones jaroches from Veracruz, to stir the feet,
Voices, to catch your heart in your throat.

Mexico, who opens her front-door to tourists and foreigners in exile;
While through her back-door, to do or die, pushes those she can no
    longer feed.

And so we meet,
My dark-eyed friend, of the cheeky smile and the agile mind,
the musical soul and the dancing feet
In the *casa* of Jenny and Juan,
The bustling apartment on Acapulco Street,
The unofficial Australian Embassy.
The starting point for our journeys together.

MÉXICO A CHALMA

Chalma, Easter 1978
With Sergio and Rosa,
We four Leftists set out

For Chalma
Three hours by car,
By knee, many dusty kilometres,
And some crawled in penance all the way,
To 'go to heaven clean'.

Chalma – southern cardinal point in the Aztec religion.
Christian flagellation, pain and penitence
Indian celebration – the ritual, the dance.

'Music was bound up with the dance and the dance with religion; all forms of religious expression involved dancing. It was part of the collective hypnotism; the evolutions of the dancer and the ornaments, and the furiously rapid movements robbed all of their self-possession and gave them the feeling that their needs – for which the dance was designed – had been supplied. Masks and costumes were important in these dances and they have survived to a surprising degree among the Indians of the present day.'

Green foil aglitter on his eyelids,
A wicked glint from within,
One defiant old local blocked the camera's way.
Este festival no es para las turistas!
This is not a festival for tourists!
'Our dance is sacred!'
'Photos cost!'
For the novices,
Children and first-timers, like ourselves,
Yellow flowers woven into crowns.

The procession seemed to have turned purple
With the mauve perfume of the incense.
As though its scent

Had taken on the colour
Of the aura of its official bearer,
A dignified, grey-haired woman
In soft feathery head-dress,
And tunic of mauve and gold.

In a wayside stall,
Christ winked from his cross
On a 3D post card.

Silver paper and bright coloured cloths,
The final touches to the massive wooden crosses,
On the ground, where they lay
Waiting to be borne
Heavenward, to the hills.

Huarache-clad feet
With anklets of dried nuts:
'the bones of the priest – *huesos del fraile*'
After those who had come to conquer and convert.

Feet stomping, nuts shaking,
Prayer and penance, bones breaking.

On swirling cloaks of red and gold,
Christs undulate
From sequined crosses
That shimmer and shake,
On backgrounds aglitter
With embroidered designs in braid and bead,
Of Aztec symbols
And Christian texts.

Aqua and silver
Iridescent pink,
Spangles and mirrors
Flash through the dance.

Plumed heads bob and wave.
The old, eyes closed with tradition's self-assurance,
The young, with youth's uncertainty
Preen themselves self-consciously.

Feet stomping, nuts shaking,
Prayer and penance, bones breaking.
Concheros strum the dance of the shell.
Bombas awaken the demons from hell.

And the feet set the beat,
With the shivering sound,
Of the 'bones of the priests',
As they whirl round and round.

Feet stomping, nuts shaking,
Prayer and penance, bones breaking.
Concheros strum the dance of the shell.
Bombas awaken the demons from hell.

México, México, pobre México. ¡Tan lejos de dios, tan cerca de los
 Estados Unidos!
The Hotel Riviera,
Adobe huts and clothes lines in its yard.

The Medical Centre,
With its rubble waiting room.

The gold-plated church,
The palace of God –
'Come to me you who are worn and weary,
And I will ease your burden.'

Long live the Virgin, immune to all Earthly Delights,
Save, immaculate conception, ecclesiastical deception!

And the feet, set the beat,
With the shivering sound,
Of the 'bones of the priests', as they whirl, round and round.

And the feet, set the beat,
With the shivering sound,
Of the 'bones of the priests', as they whirl, round and round.

And the feet, set the beat,
With the shivering sound,
Of the 'bones of the priests', as they whirl, round and round.

EVITA, O SIMPLEMENTE ELLA

Another first for us both.
In a little old church in Coyoacán
A split-level show, on a split-level stage
Outrage!?
'Webber and Rice', spiked with Mexican spice
¡*Bien picante!*

An all-male production
Of the Show, of the Song, of the Country –
'Don't Cry For Me'.

Evita strutting her stuff,
Playing the whore,
Friend of the poor?
Till death do us snuff –
Mi amor.

GAY DISCO

1978
The show: Evita
The dance: *a la Travolta*
The movie: *Saturday Night Fever.*

Don't cry for me, 'Cos I'm Stayin' Alive, Stayin' Alive,
Don't cry for me, 'Cos I'm Stayin' Alive, Stayin' Alive,
Dancing out my passions in this glitzy dive.
Glitzy dive
G.D.
Gay Disco.
M.D.F. México Distrito Federal. México la Capital.
The glitzy disco
Was not doing great dollars
When we walked in,
So we got down and cumbia'd,
Till the *fiebre de sábado en la noche*
Set us all sweating and twitching *a la Travolta.*

'The songs were repeated endlessly, monotonously; and the furiously rapid movements robbed all of their self-possession and gave them a feeling that their needs – for which the dance was designed – had been supplied.'

Left, Latin and gay,
Not exactly the number-one combination
In Colombia, Mexico, or, north of the border.

From Mexico to New York.
'Mexico, Mexico, poor Mexico.
So far from God,
So near to the United States.'

From Autonomous Mexico University
Brilliant student, and patient teacher of Marxist Economics, to New
    York, New York.
The Big Apple of Temptation
In the Garden of Sky-Scrapers:
'Taste me. Try me. You'll be hooked on me forever!'
New York, New York,
The Thorn
Which bleeds the Mexican Cactus dry.
New York, New York, *'donde la libertad es una estatua'*.
New York, New York, where liberty is a statue.

NEW YORK

From Sundays in Chapultepec,
To Mondays in Central Park.
From Mayan marvels in the Museum of Anthropology
To 'Guernica' on loan, in the Museum of Modern Art.
From scaling the stairways to the sun – the pyramids at Teotihuacán,
To swirling down the spirals of the Guggenheim
'Fuck Art, Let's Skate!'
Taking in the aesthetics on the slide down.

Taking photos of each other in the alcoves.
From gyrating to the beat of the latest North American dance craze –
    in a gay bar in Mexico,
To steaming to the sensual sounds of salsa, in a Latin bar in New
    York, to the music of Tito Puente and Willie Colon.
Me, changing partners
From you, to your friend, all night,
So you could stay on the dance floor together.

It's 1978. You still have to wait.
To get the OK, to dance and be gay.

CAUTION – UN

From New York, one photo.
The caption: CAUTION WATCH YOUR STEP.

Outside the United Nations building
On a windy construction site,
Watched by two smiling workers,
You took the photo of me,
My crutch planted in an arch
Over their Safety-First placard –
'Caution, watch your step.'

A sign? A warning?
Or just us, setting up
Silly shots?

'No regrets. *Rien de rien*,' you say.
You stayed.

From giving classes,
To four years washing glasses,
Then four happy years
Teaching
History and economics
In Spanish and English.

And so we meet again.
It's late autumn '86.

We share your split-level apartment for two weeks.
We look, we smile, we cry, we talk, and talk, and talk.
We don't dance; we embrace.
I love you Jeannie. I love you Hector, very much.

Your split-level, 6 by 20 apartment, next door to La Mode Dry
    Cleaners
A sign-post opposite:
IT'S THE LAW
CLEAN UP AFTER YOUR DOG
MAXIMUM FINE, $100.00.

On seeing a photo of this,
Some young friends in Mexico burst into giggles
'$100.00 for the *caca* of your *perro* –
 Must be pedigree pooh!'

Your split-level apartment,
Your space with taste,
Your home with a heart.

Your bed and some of your many books on the top level
Reached by a ladder, steep like a ship's stairway.

Below, the study, kitchen, dining and bathroom, the guest room,
Where I spent some anxious nights,
My feet tapping in time with the refrigerator's motor,
My head making contact with the TV.
Fear of short circuiting?

We go to a great Cuban restaurant,
Frijoles, rice, liver and coffee – $5.00!
With Morris, for a wet afternoon stroll in Central Park,
'Round Midnight'
And then an inspection of his elaborate theatre and fantastical puppets.

We catch up on each other's expanding musical catalogues;
Beside Ruben Blades, Bartok, Beethoven and The Beatles
Sondheim now rolls merrily along.

The 'Tongues-Out' post card collection begins:
The instigator, a cheeky Einstein on his 50th birthday – in black and white.
Tongue out.
Followed by,
Four frightful pink, and luminous green punks –
'Welcome to New York.'
Tongues out.
The latest addition,
Your Mexican Tiger Mask, in papier-mâché, yellow, red and black
Tongue out,
Pulls a face at me, from my blue kitchen wall at Maroubra.

BUEN VIAJE

And now you're going to Machu Picchu.
A pilgrimage,
Different from our other sojourns of discovery, decadence and dance.
A journey through mists and mystery, to the hitching place of the sun.
A journey back, to the origins of your continent, to your spiritual
    source and centre
A quest.

A moral reinforcement.

May the sun's golden rays warm you.
May Your Gods answer your prayers.
May Machu Picchu work her magic for you.

It's a tough climb, they say, but well worth the effort.
And, if you're too tired to tango,
I'll be dancing for you, *querido compañero*.

I love you Hector. Te quiero Héctor.

Land of corn

Jacqueline Buswell

Quetzalcóatl, feathered serpent god
became an ant trawled the mountains
to retrieve a grain that he gave to the people

this was a gift from the morning star
the first cob was a tiny vial of seed
not like today's giant ears

corn was planted with beans and squash
and for protection from demons:
orange and yellow flowers

species later confirmed by science to hold
pesticidal properties

the crop
tilled by hand and hoe
harvested with a firm turn of the wrist

the grain
ground on stone by two strong arms
or carried to the mill each morning

the dough
shaped by folding clapping hands
placed on the griddle and turned

one tortilla at a time
hot to the fingers

colonial land grabs   mining   sugar cane
forced many cornfields to steep hillsides
laws called land reform
never served the small farmer

free trade only made things worse
corn imported from the northern neighbour
is of inferior quality
but the market rules

the many coloured cobs of Mexico
are further threatened by
genetic engineering
and a powerful seed monopoly

children of the corn civilization
are now eating tortillas
manufactured from packaged flour

and women who grew up
in local corn economies
follow their menfolk across the border

to work perhaps in toxic
cash crop productions – tomato   tobacco
or in sweat shops

they take their gods and goddesses with them
but even gods need a certain warmth to prosper
just as a future needs a past

today the museum is the temple
Chicomecóatl   Seven Serpent corn goddess
sits back on her heels   hands on her knees

cobs of corn hang down her back
golden beads against the dark plaits
in basalt

it seems she has just straightened
from grinding the sacred maize

> Published in *Poetry & Place Anthology 2015*,
> Close-up Books Melbourne.

White rabbits

Jenny Pollak

A shaft of sunlight falls diagonally
in front of us
across the corridor.
He points towards it.
Look, he whispers,
transfigured by the sight,
as if he too were full of light. Look!

But all I see is how meagre the light is.
How it cuts through
the antiseptic glass
of the nursing home window
like a razor,
slicing through curtains,
bleeding
onto the mean
linoleum.

He looks up at me then, his face alight,
the subversive fire still burning in his eyes
after all these years.

And I am full of wonder,
not of the light,
but of him.

The wardens patrol the corridors
looking for fires
to put out.
But the inmates are wily –
they hide their fires in the corners
of their gowns or wedge them down
the sides of their chairs:

the sick and elderly
still capable of remembering
their lives
bigger than the reduction
perpetrated here.

The wardens have been hired for the size
of their hands.
They know how to put out fires –
they've been trained with the bare minimum
of their wage. They know how
to strangle rabbits.

But my love is a magician
and pulls his rabbits from thin air.

Between

Jenny Pollak

Today I can grieve. Slung like an eye
between two centuries.
Years like poultices.

I think of shadows as indulgences
we tried not to get lost in.
Better to follow the slant of a transitory light.

Your smile when it came was so deep
your head fell back when you laughed.
All the shadows were behind you.

The expats

Ruth Adler

> 'I am sure glad I live on this side of the wall.'
> *Mary Lynn*

Ever since I was a child I have had a yearning to be elsewhere. Driving through the Sydney streets at night in my parents' car, I would peer briefly into lit-up houses and see the lives of others. I would see a painting, some furniture, a fire place, a couple having dinner, young children... and, for a moment, I would want to be them, to have their lives.

As a young adult, all I wanted was to be somewhere else, to be someone else. This yearning took me on a journey which included a stint in academia and a career of almost 27 years in the Department of Foreign Affairs and Trade (DFAT). At age 24, I went to live in Mexico to undertake research for my PhD and stayed almost three years. It broke my heart to leave. Many years later I was posted to Mexico and I was sad, but not broken-hearted, to leave. By that time, I had a life to return to in Australia and, as a diplomat, one is always on the outside, a passing observer of life in the country where one is posted. In my 20s, all I wanted was to be able live in Mexico long-term; by the time I was in my late 30s I no longer felt that way.

In 2016, having recently left DFAT, I decided to revisit the country which had captivated me in my youth. My pretext was the *Under the Volcano* writing workshop, held annually in Tepoztlán, a town one and a half hours south of Mexico City by road, known for its pleasant climate, cobbled streets, historical buildings and colourful shops, markets and restaurants. From being a quiet weekend retreat for many *chilangos*,[1] over the years it had become a mecca for artists, writers and those seeking a different life or perhaps to escape a past life. Tepoztlán, *pueblo mágico* – one of Mexico's magical towns.

My visit to Tepoztlán coincided with the inauguration of President Donald Trump. Trump's planned wall along the United States-Mexican border was a hot topic, with many Mexicans and foreigners vocal in their opinion that the wall was a racist and hostile act against Mexico. I wondered whether the election of Trump would lead to an exodus of United States citizens looking for a better life south of the border.

I decided I would like to find out and set about to talk to some US citizens who had made their home in Tepoztlán. The phenomenon of people coming from the United States to Mexico – sometimes called 'reverse migration' – was not new. Mexico had always attracted adventurers from the United States and other foreigners wishing to establish a new life. It had also – at times – been a place of refuge for foreigners, with many coming from the United States to Mexico in the 1950s to flee McCarthyism and in the 1960s and 1970s to escape the Vietnam war draft.

With this in mind, I was surprised and somewhat disconcerted to discover that the first person I met was a Trump supporter. What on earth was a Trump supporter doing in Tepoztlán? I met Bill at a literary event at the popular *La Sombra del Sabino* bookshop café[2] at which the group adopted a declaration to protest the 'belligerent attacks' on writers and journalists by President-elect Trump. Bill sat on the edge of the event, with his arms folded. As each writer addressed the group, Bill shook his head. In Bill's world people divided into two camps:

---

[1] People from Mexico City.
[2] http://lasombradelsabino.com.mx.

business people, who supported Trump ('we fretted over whether he would get elected'), and others, government workers, teachers, writers, and artists – Clinton supporters. Bill fervently believed in Trump:

'I believe wholeheartedly that Trump will rebuild America and that, unlike the Clintons, Trump is an honest politician who tells the truth, even when it makes people feel uncomfortable... Sometimes I feel like he is sticking his foot in his mouth, but... he seems to be learning now to be more political. He is not prejudiced – his business organisation is staffed with minorities; they say he's tough, but he's fair...'

Bill had come to Mexico to retire, after many years of running two businesses in Texas. At age 73, he was a large man and walked with a stick. He had sold his businesses in 2007, just before the global financial crisis of 2008 and drove to Mexico in a van. His adult children thought he was mad. 'Why are you going to that dangerous place?' they had asked.

'I came to Mexico because I wanted somewhere I could afford to live and... I had been coming to for many years and... I really liked the place... I found a Spanish class I liked and then I met a woman, Julieta', he told me.

Julieta ran a popular bakery in town which supported her extended family. The bakery had done well, although it had been affected by a hike in the price of butter, following the devaluation of the Mexican peso in the wake of Trump's election. They lived in a small brick house, which was part of a small gated complex of dwellings occupied by his landlord and members of Julieta's family. Bill spent his days reading and watching the news on the internet and pottering around at home or in the town. He was, however, health conscious and had engaged a personal trainer who worked with him to increase his fitness and mobility. His bookshelf was full of books on health and alternative medicine, in which he took a strong interest. In common with Trump, Bill was an 'anti-vaxxer' – opposed to the compulsory vaccination of children and believing that this has caused a global epidemic of autism.

By contrast, Susan – who ran *La Sombra del Sabino* – like many other expats in Tepoztlán, was deeply disappointed about the election of Trump.

'It's way more than disappointing, it's devastating,' she lamented.

Originally from Los Angeles, Susan had studied speech pathology and audiology. She met her Mexican husband Tomás, who was studying to be in architect, in the US. They married and eventually moved to Mexico.

'I insisted [to Tomás] that I would like to live in Mexico and I wanted to know my Mexican family... and to be bilingual as well', she said.

They initially lived in Mexico City, where Tomás worked as an architect and Susan in speech pathology. They started coming to Tepoztlán and Susan fell in love with the town. Tomás was reluctant to come at first because he felt it would be difficult to work remotely from Tepoztlán. They rented a house and, for a while, Tomás worked in Mexico City during the week and came to Tepoztlán on weekends. They were thankful to be able to adopt two beautiful children. Eventually they found a plot of land they loved and built a house, where Susan lived with their children.

Susan initially worked in her field, and later, following an extended period in the US caring for her dying mother, she returned to Mexico. Two friends of hers decided to start a café and invited Susan to join them. They rented a run-down house with a large garden and *La Sombra del Sabino* was born.

Were there things she does not like about the town or Mexico? A sad expression came over her face. Once a teacher had said to her adopted son, 'you could be selling *chicle* in the street'. Another child told him, 'you are like a rat from the drain'.

Did she intend to stay in Mexico?

'The United States has changed. I don't even recognise my country.'

Mary Lynn was another North American expat who had no intention of leaving soon.

'I am sure glad I live on this side of the wall,' she smiled.

She was equally disappointed in the election of Trump, but generous in her comments:

'I don't want to set the Trump administration in such a negative frame that he seems to be setting it in... but it is difficult to be hopeful for someone who does not have awareness of their international impact.'

Like many other North Americans in Mexico she voted in the November election.

'I am not going to share who I voted for... but she didn't win.'

Mary Lynn had lived in Mexico for nine years. Originally from Texas, she had completed a PhD in counselling psychology. She later moved to Colorado and got a real estate licence and taught skiing. She started to come to Mexico and bought a place in Baja California. A lover of nature and being outdoors, she could indulge her passion for cycling and hiking in Mexico. Eventually, she fell in love with an American living in Mexico and moved to Mexico City. She had initially lived in the La Condesa neighbourhood, known for its art deco architecture and bars and cafes.

Mary Lynn lived alone in a large modern colonial style house on the road from Tepoztlán to Amatlán with sweeping views of the mountains and valley. The house was, however, too big for her and she was trying to sell it. She had bought another lot where she planned to build another house and 'down-size'. Living in Baja California had taught her about water conservation and solar energy.

Had Mexico changed? For Mary Lynn, not much had changed, but she said she was more aware of what is going on in Mexico, than she had been ten years earlier.

And would she stay?

'Well, I got my Mexican passport... I was ecstatic,' she told me.

Towards the end of my time, I met Don. Don was a self-described college dropout and told me he had divorced and suffered mental health problems when he was younger. Originally from Syracuse, New York, he came to Mexico in search of a new life and was thriving, living outside of Tepoztlán. He had eked out a simple life-style, camping or living by the generosity of friends. He had been captivated by the spirituality of the area and the honest warmth of ordinary Mexicans, which he had experienced in abundance. He was, however, fearful that the election of Trump might turn the tide of national feeling against North Americans. Acutely aware of this, he had joined with other foreigners to show their solidarity with Mexicans and to develop sustainable projects for the local community, and was living under the radar.

Another person living under the radar – or more correctly off-the-grid – was Baru, who had originally come to Mexico with the nomadic theatre group known as 'The Illuminated Elephants', which had settled in Mexico and established what today is known as the eco-village of Huehuecoyotl. Baru was another who was in search of meaning when he first came to Mexico, almost 40 years previously. These days he lived in a remote area out of town and practised as an artist and carpenter. His Mexican wife was a healer, well-known in the town. For Baru, the US was another world and there was no possibility he would ever want to return.

As I prepared to leave and return to my life in Australia, I reflected on my brief encounter with this other world of the North American expat in Mexico. While I had lived in a number of countries on various postings over the years and met many expats, I was struck by the openness and willingness of all whom I met to share their experiences – their generosity of spirit, both towards me and towards Mexico. While they came from different backgrounds, they shared a love of Mexico and Tepoztlán, the place they now called home. I felt the strong pull of Mexico and wanted to change places. The urge and yearning to be somewhere else…

Journeys. Australian Women in Mexico,
compiled and edited by Ruth Adler, Jacqueline Buswell and Jenny Cooper.

www.ingramcontent.com/pod-product-compliance
Lightning Source LLC
Chambersburg PA
CBHW020321010526
44107CB00054B/1923